MAFF

**Ministry of Agriculture
Fisheries and Food**

Household Food Consumption and Expenditure 1990

with a study of trends over the period
1940-1990

Annual Report of the National
Food Survey Committee

LONDON : HMSO

© Crown Copyright 1991
Applications for reproduction
should be made to HMSO

First published 1991

ISBN 0 11 242910 6

The National Food Survey Committee

R E MORDUE, BSc, MS
Ministry of Agriculture, Fisheries and Food, Chairman

J A BEAUMONT, BSc, PhDS
Institute of Grocery Distribution

MARGARET R BONE, BSocSc
Office of Population Censuses and Surveys

PROFESSOR A CHESHER, BSocSc
University of Bristol

M E KNOWLES, BPharm, PhD, CChem, FRSC, FIFST
Ministry of Agriculture, Fisheries and Food

PROFESSOR C RITSON, BA, MAgricSc
University of Newcastle upon Tyne

ROSALIND SKINNER, MBBS, MD, MSc, MFPHM
Scottish Office, Home and Health Department

J M SLATER, BSc, MS, PhD
Ministry of Agriculture, Fisheries and Food

R G WHITEHEAD, BSc, PhD, MA, FIBiol
MRC Dunn Nutrition Group

M J WISEMAN, MB, MRCP
Department of Health

LESLEY YEOMANS, BSc, PhD
Tate and Lyle

Secretaries

D H BUSS, PhD, FIFST
Ministry of Agriculture, Fisheries and Food

SHEILA M DIXON, BSc
Ministry of Agriculture, Fisheries and Food

Preface

This edition of the National Food Survey Committee's Annual Report marks the fiftieth year of the Survey. The first Report of the Committee was published in 1951 and presented results from 1940 to 1949. Subsequent reports have been produced more or less annually since then, giving detailed analyses of household food purchases and expenditure for the latest full year of the Survey. This volume presents the 1990 results and examines the nutritional value of the diet. In addition, it illustrates some of the wealth of the data collected over the fifty years in a section dealing with long term trends in the purchasing patterns and diet of British households.

This historical perspective is timely as the Committee looks forward to implementing the recommendations of its 1989 review of certain aspects of the Survey. Confectionery and alcoholic drinks are to be included among the foods already recorded by all Survey households from 1992. At the same time selected households will also provide information on food purchased or consumed away from home.

The Committee wishes to record its thanks to the many households who have provided information for the Survey. In addition thanks are due to the staff of the Social Survey Division of the Office of Population, Censuses and Surveys, who selected the samples and provided much helpful advice, and of the British Market Research Bureau who carried out the fieldwork. Overall responsibility for the Survey and for the processing of the results rests with the Ministry of Agriculture, Fisheries and Food.

R E Mordue
(Chairman National Food Survey Committee)

Contents

Page

List of Tables and Figures   ix

Section 1   Introduction   1

Section 2   Results of the 1990 Survey
     National Averages   3
     Regional Comparisons   12
     Income Group Comparisons   16
     Household Composition Comparisons   21
     Household Composition Groups within Income Groups   25

Section 3   Nutritional Results
     National Averages   29
     Regional, Household Composition and Income Group Differences   32

Section 4   Analysis of Historical Data from the Survey
     Background   33
     Trends in Household Food Consumption and Expenditure   33
     Regional Comparisons   40
     Income Group Comparisons   43
     Household Composition Comparisons   47
     Seasonality   50
     Convenience Foods   52
     Free Food   54
     Nutrient Intakes   55

Appendix A - Structure of the Survey   57
Appendix B - Supplementary Tables   65
Appendix C - Tables of Historical Data   92
Glossary and Additional Information   116

List of Tables and Figures

Page

1. Introduction

Table 1.1   Consumers' expenditure in the United Kingdom   2

Figure 1.2   Consumers' expenditure at constant prices   2

Figure 1.3   Retail prices for food and other items   2

2. Results of the 1990 Survey

Table 2.1   Household food expenditure and total value of food obtained for consumption   3

Figure 2.2   Changes in expenditure, prices and real value of food, compared with 1989   3

Table 2.3   Consumption and expenditure for main food groups   4

Table 2.4   Composition of household food expenditure   5

Table 2.5   Consumption and expenditure for milk and cheese   5

Table 2.6   Consumption and expenditure for meat, fish and eggs   6

Table 2.7   Consumption and expenditure for fats   7

Table 2.8   Consumption and expenditure for sugar and preserves   7

Table 2.9   Consumption and expenditure for vegetables and fruit   8

Table 2.10   Consumption and expenditure for bread and cereal products   9

Table 2.11   Consumption and expenditure for beverages and miscellaneous foods   9

Table 2.12   Purchases and expenditure for soft drinks   10

Table 2.13   Number of meals out (not from household supply)   10

Table 2.14   Expenditure on household food and on meals bought away from the home   11

Figure 2.15   Average number of mid-day meals per week per child aged 5-14 years   11

Table 2.16   Expenditure and consumption for selected foods by region, 1990   13

Figure 2.17   Consumption of fish by region, 1990   14

Figure 2.18   Consumption of cereals by region, 1990   15

Figure 2.19   Consumption of fresh fruit by region, 1990   15

Table 2.20   Expenditure and consumption for selected foods by income group, 1990   16

Figure 2.21 Consumption and expenditure for fats according to income group, 1990   18

Figure 2.22 Consumption and expenditure for sugar and preserves according to income group, 1990   19

Figure 2.23 Consumption and expenditure for fruit according to income group, 1990   20

Table 2.24 Consumption of selected foods by household composition, 1990   21

Figure 2.25 Household food expenditure on main food groups per person by number of people in adult-only households, 1990   22

Figure 2.26 Household food expenditure on main food groups per person by number ofchildren in 2-adult households, 1990   22

Figure 2.27 Expenditure on fresh fruit by household composition, 1990   23

Figure 2.28 Expenditure on sugar and preserves by household composition, 1990   24

Figure 2.29 Expenditure on bread by household composition, 1990   24

Figure 2.30 Total household food expenditure per head by certain   household composition groups within income groups, 1990   25

Figure 2.31 Expenditure on selected foods by certain household composition groups within income groups, 1990   26

3. Nutritional Results

Table 3.1 Energy value of household food, drinks and confectionery   29

Table 3.2 Proportions of household food energy derived from fat, protein and carbohydrate   30

Table 3.3 Household intakes of minerals and vitamins expressed as percentages of recommended amounts or reference intakes   31

Table 3.4 Selected nutritional results by region, income group and in households with 2 adults and different numbers of children in 1990   32

4. Analysis of Historical Data from the Survey

Table 4.1 Household food expenditure and total value of food obtained for consumption   34

Figure 4.2 Expenditure on household food as a percentage of total household expenditure   34

Figure 4.3 Percentage of household food expenditure on main food groups   35

Figure 4.4 Consumption of bread   35

Figure 4.5 Consumption of fats   36

Figure 4.6 Consumption of milk and milk products 37

Figure 4.7 Consumption of meats 37

Figure 4.8 Consumption of fruit 38

Figure 4.9 Consumption of vegetables 39

Figure 4.10 Regions for analysis 41

Figure 4.11 Vegetable consumption by region, 1960 and 1990 41

Figure 4.12 Fat consumption by region, 1960 and 1990 42

Table 4.13 Income groups in 1952 43

Table 4.14 Income groups in 1990 43

Figure 4.15 Expenditure on main food groups by income group, 1952 and 1990 44

Figure 4.16 Consumption of milk and cream by income group 45

Figure 4.17 Consumption of eggs by income group 45

Figure 4.18 Consumption of sugar and preserves by income group 46

Figure 4.19 Consumption of fruit and fruit products by income group 46

Figure 4.20 Expenditure per person on all household food by number of people in adult-only households 47

Figure 4.21 Expenditure per person on meat and meat products in adult-only households 48

Figure 4.22 Expenditure per person on fish in adult-only households 48

Figure 4.23 Expenditure per person on all household food in 2-adult households with children 49

Figure 4.24 Expenditure per person on eggs in 2-adult households with children 49

Figure 4.25 Expenditure per person on fruit in 2-adult households with children 50

Figure 4.26 Seasonal variation in consumption of eggs 51

Figure 4.27 Seasonal variation in consumption of fresh vegetables 51

Figure 4.28 Seasonal variation in consumption of apples 52

Figure 4.29 Consumption of canned and bottled convenience foods 53

Figure 4.30 Consumption of frozen convenience foods 53

Figure 4.31 Consumption of other convenience foods 54

Figure 4.32 Value of 'free food' as a percentage of total value of all food 54

Figure 4.33 Nutritional value of household food supplies 55

Figure 4.34 Percentage of energy from carbohydrate, fat and protein 56

Section 1

Introduction

This Report marks the 50th anniversary of the National Food Survey, which was set up in 1940 to monitor the adequacy of the diet of urban households, and is now a modern, authoritative survey of domestic food consumption. The Report presents data derived from the 1990 Survey together with an analysis of selected trends over the previous fifty years.

During the course of 1990, 7,205 randomly selected private households throughout Great Britain took part in the National Food Survey. Each participating household recorded details of all items of food brought into the home for human consumption during the course of a week. Information on soft drinks bought into the home was also recorded, although it is not included in the main analysis of the Survey data. Like alcoholic drinks and confectionery, for which no information is yet collected, these items are frequently bought without the knowledge of the main record-keeper. The numbers of meals eaten outside the home were recorded, but not the content or cost of such meals. Information on these items will be collected more fully from 1992, when households will record alcoholic drink and confectionery purchases into household supplies. In addition, members of selected households will record details of food, alcoholic drinks, soft drinks and confectionery consumed outside the home.

The main results for 1990 are set out in Section 2, showing consumption and expenditure data for major types of food for the nation as a whole, and according to various household characteristics. These analyses provide valuable insights into the consumption and expenditure patterns of different types of household. Information on the number of meals eaten out and purchases of soft drinks is also presented in this Section. Section 3 contains more detailed nutritional information for 1990. In this report, Section 4 presents a special analysis of fifty years of data from the Survey showing trends in patterns of consumption and expenditure. Details of the structure and conduct of the survey and of the nutritional analysis are set out in Appendix A. Appendix B contains supplementary tables showing the main 1990 results, and Appendix C has further historical tables.

Consumers' total expenditure on food and drink amounted to an estimated £83 billion in 1990. Of this, an estimated £42 billion was spent on household food (Table 1.1). To put this in its historical context, Figure 1.2 shows quite dramatically how household food expenditure has risen very little in real terms over the last 40 years, while total consumers' expenditure has risen by some 180 per cent over the same period. Expenditure on household food represented only 12 per cent of total consumer expenditure in 1990, compared with 26 per cent in 1950. Some allowance must of course be made for additional

1

expenditure on meals outside the home, which will have been a more significant factor in recent years.

Table 1.1
Consumers' expenditure in the United Kingdom

	1980		1985		1990	
	£ b	%	£ b	%	£ b	%
Household expenditure on food[a]	23.7	16.9	30.7	14.1	41.8	12.0
Expenditure on meals out[b]	6.0	4.3	9.2	4.2	19.7	5.6
Total expenditure on food	29.7	21.2	39.9	18.3	61.5	17.6
Alcoholic drink[a]	10.0	7.2	15.6	7.2	21.7	6.2
Total food and drink	39.7	28.4	55.5	25.5	83.2	23.8
Total consumers' expenditure	139.6	100.0	217.6	100.0	349.4	100.0

(a) Central Statistical Office
(b) Ministry of Agriculture, Fisheries and Food estimates

Figure 1.2
Consumers' expenditure at constant prices

—— Total expenditure

—— Household food expenditure

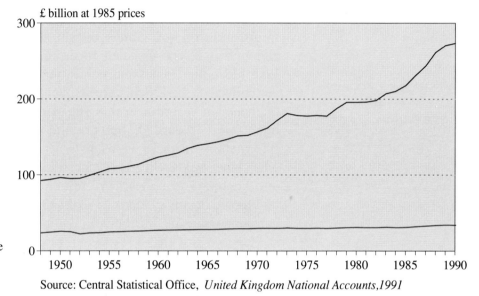

Source: Central Statistical Office, *United Kingdom National Accounts, 1991*

Figure 1.3 shows that, especially since 1970, food prices have risen more slowly than prices in general. This is a factor in the smaller proportion of income needed for household food supplies.

Figure 1.3
Retail prices for food and for other items

—— Other items

—— Food

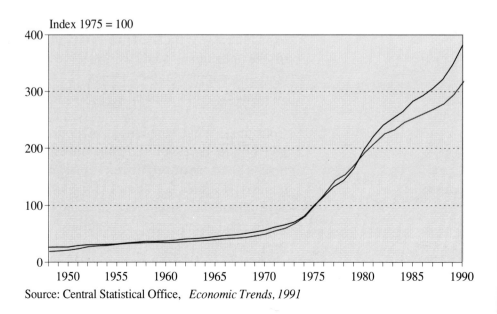

Source: Central Statistical Office, *Economic Trends, 1991*

Section 2

Results of the 1990 Survey

Average household food expenditure in each quarter of 1990 was higher than in the corresponding quarter of 1989, resulting in an overall increase for the year of 5.4 per cent (Table 2.1). The value of consumption, including the value of garden and allotment produce, was estimated at £12.35 per person per week in 1990, compared with £11.73 in the previous year.

Table 2.1
Household food expenditure and total value of food obtained for consumption

per person per week

	Expenditure on food			Value of garden and allotment produce, etc [a]		Value of consumption [b]		
	1989	1990	Change	1989	1990	1989	1990	Change
	£	£	%	£	£	£	£	%
1st quarter	11.05	11.68	+5.7	0.16	0.22	11.21	11.90	+6.2
2nd quarter	11.85	12.59	+6.2	0.16	0.18	12.01	12.77	+6.3
3rd quarter	11.34	11.95	+5.4	0.34	0.30	11.68	12.25	+4.9
4th quarter	11.75	12.28	+4.5	0.27	0.24	12.02	12.52	+4.2
Yearly average	**11.50**	**12.12**	**+5.4**	**0.23**	**0.23**	**11.73**	**12.35**	**+5.3**

(a)   valued at average prices paid by housewives for comparable purchases

(b)   expenditure on food purchased for consumption in the home, plus the value of garden and allotment produce, etc

Prices paid for household food in 1990 averaged 8.9 per cent more than in 1989. As a result, the estimated real value of food purchased fell by 3.2 per cent. Within this total, seasonal and convenience foods showed the largest increases in average prices (Figure 2.2). Details

Figure 2.2
Changes in expenditure, prices and real value of food, compared with 1989

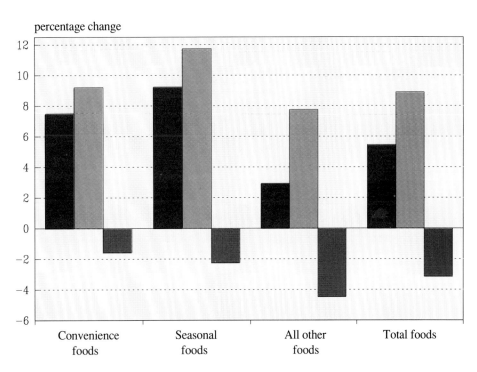

■ Expenditure
▨ Prices
▨ Real value of food purchased

3

of the average prices paid for individual food items are given in Appendix B Table 2[1].

National Averages

The 1990 results indicate a decline in household consumption of most of the major groups of foods since 1988 (Table 2.3), with the exception of fish. To some extent, these changes reflect a trend towards purchase of more highly processed or prepared foods, such as trimmed and boned meat, trimmed vegetables, and 'convenience foods' which are ready to heat and serve, all of which have less wastage. The results are also affected by the number of meals and snacks eaten outside the home. The largest proportional decreases in consumption were for eggs, fats and oils and sugar and preserves. Over the same period, expenditure rose for all food groups, with marked increases for fish, fruit and vegetables, and miscellaneous foods. Consumption and expenditure patterns within all these groups are considered in more detail in the following paragraphs, and detailed quarterly results can be found in Appendix B Table 1.

Table 2.3
Consumption and expenditure for main food groups

						per person per week
	Consumption			Expenditure		
	1988	1989	1990	1988	1989	1990
	(ounces) [(a)]			(pence)		
Milk and cream (pt or eq pt)	4.01	3.93	3.82	112.46	120.85	127.69
Cheese	4.13	4.07	4.00	38.21	40.01	41.43
Meat and meat products	36.59	35.94	34.11	303.65	327.91	337.24
Fish	5.06	5.20	5.08	57.63	63.09	66.62
Eggs (no)	2.67	2.29	2.20	19.32	17.75	19.49
Fats and oils	9.86	9.48	9.00	34.51	36.10	36.11
Sugar and preserves	8.79	8.22	7.73	17.77	17.65	18.08
Fruit and vegetables	115.01	114.41	111.35	226.99	243.07	266.58
Cereals (incl. bread)	54.12	53.33	51.79	180.17	191.86	203.98
Beverages	2.66	2.60	2.47	42.34	43.19	43.18
Other foods	–	–	–	43.63	48.20	51.66
All foods	–	–	–	£10.77	£11.50	£12.12

(a) except where otherwise stated

The composition of total expenditure in 1990 is illustrated in Figure 2.4.

---

1 It should be noted that since the results for household consumption presented in this Report include both purchases and 'free food', average prices paid cannot in general be derived by dividing the expenditure on a particular food by average consumption.

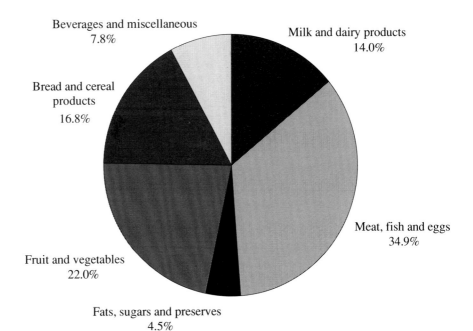

Figure 2.4
Composition of household food expenditure

Beverages and miscellaneous
7.8%

Milk and dairy products
14.0%

Bread and cereal products
16.8%

Meat, fish and eggs
34.9%

Fruit and vegetables
22.0%

Fats, sugars and preserves
4.5%

Milk, Cream and Cheese

Total household consumption of milk and cream declined by 5 per cent between 1988 and 1990 to 3.82 pints per person, of which 3.41 pints was liquid milk. Within this, as Table 2.5 shows, the continuing trend towards low fat milks is very noticeable. Consumption of liquid wholemilk fell by nearly a fifth, while consumption of low fat and reduced fat milks rose by a third. Yoghurt consumption continues to grow, and was worth about 17 pence per person per week in 1990. Consumption of cheese declined slightly over this period, to an average of 4 ounces per person per week.

Table 2.5
Consumption and expenditure for milk and cheese

		Consumption			Expenditure		
		1988	1989	1990	1988	1989	1990
		(ounces)[a]			(pence)		
MILK AND CREAM:							
Liquid wholemilk, full price	(pt)	2.60	2.37	2.12	65.62	64.57	61.80
Welfare and school milk	(pt)	0.05	0.05	0.04	0.11	0.10	0.12
Low fat milks	(pt)	0.93	1.09	1.25	23.29	29.52	36.23
Yoghurt	(pt)	0.16	0.16	0.17	12.55	14.09	16.55
Dried and other milk[b]	(pt or eq pt)	0.25	0.22	0.21	7.07	8.26	8.99
Cream	(pt)	0.03	0.03	0.02	3.82	4.30	4.00
Total milk and cream		**4.01**	**3.93**	**3.82**	**112.46**	**120.85**	**127.69**
CHEESE:							
Natural		3.84	3.76	3.70	35.17	36.47	37.72
Processed		0.29	0.31	0.30	3.04	3.54	3.71
Total cheese		**4.13**	**4.07**	**4.00**	**38.21**	**40.01**	**41.43**

per person per week

(a) except where otherwise stated
(b) includes condensed milk

Meat, Fish and Eggs

Average expenditure on meat and meat products in 1990 was £3.37 per person per week, an increase of 3 per cent on 1989 (Table 2.6). Over the same period, amounts consumed declined by 5 per cent, reflecting in part the trend towards purchase of meat in more highly prepared or processed forms. Beef, pork and bacon and ham showed most reduction in quantities purchased, with lamb and poultry consumption little changed. Expenditure was higher in all categories except beef and veal. During the year, beef consumption was affected by publicity surrounding bovine spongiform encephalopathy (BSE) , and supplies were short and prices relatively high for pigmeat. Consumption of fish returned to an overall level similar to that in 1988, with lower amounts of fresh, processed and shell fish offset by increases in prepared and, particularly, frozen fish and fish products. Consumption of eggs averaged 2.2 per person per week, a reduction of 4 per cent compared with 1989.

Table 2.6

Consumption and expenditure for meat, fish and eggs

						per person per week
	Consumption			Expenditure		
	1988	1989	1990	1988	1989	1990
	(ounces) [a]			(pence)		
MEAT:						
Beef and veal	6.35	6.03	5.24	70.58	74.38	63.89
Mutton and lamb	2.78	2.99	2.92	24.79	27.40	28.64
Pork	3.29	3.15	2.97	26.20	27.81	29.07
Total carcase meat	**12.43**	**12.17**	**11.12**	**121.56**	**129.59**	**121.60**
Bacon and ham, uncooked	3.48	3.35	3.02	30.59	32.72	33.92
Poultry, uncooked	7.52	7.31	7.43	41.82	43.72	50.02
Other meat and meat products	13.15	13.12	12.55	109.67	121.89	131.71
Total meat	**36.59**	**35.94**	**34.11**	**303.65**	**327.91**	**337.24**
FISH:						
Fresh	1.20	1.24	1.11	13.60	14.72	15.04
Processed and shell	0.54	0.59	0.51	7.82	9.15	8.66
Prepared, including fish products	1.76	1.72	1.79	21.49	23.39	24.93
Frozen, including fish products	1.56	1.66	1.65	14.73	15.83	17.99
Total fish	**5.06**	**5.20**	**5.08**	**57.63**	**63.09**	**66.62**
EGGS (no)	2.67	2.29	2.20	19.32	17.75	19.49

(a) except where otherwise stated.

Fats

Total purchases of fats averaged 9 ounces per person per week in 1990, 5 per cent less than in 1989 but expenditure was unchanged (Table 2.7). Within this, consumption of lard and compound cooking fat showed the most marked reduction, and butter and margarine declined by 8 per cent. Average consumption of low fat and dairy spreads was stable, having risen considerably in previous years, and consumption of vegetable and salad oils rose by 6 per cent.

Table 2.7
Consumption and
expenditure for fats

						per person per week
	Consumption			Expenditure		
	1988	1989	1990	1988	1989	1990
	(ounces)			(pence)		
FATS:						
Butter	2.00	1.75	1.61	11.97	11.78	11.01
Margarine	3.78	3.47	3.19	10.09	9.90	9.97
Low fat and dairy spreads	1.35	1.60	1.58	5.97	7.44	7.89
Lard and compound cooking fat	1.00	0.89	0.80	1.98	1.91	1.80
Vegetable and salad oils	1.42	1.44	1.53	2.99	3.29	3.77
Other fats and oils	0.30	0.32	0.28	1.51	1.76	1.66
Total fats	**9.86**	**9.48**	**9.00**	**34.51**	**36.10**	**36.11**

Sugar and Preserves

Household purchases of sugar and preserves continued to decline, showing an overall reduction of 6 per cent compared with 1989 (Table 2.8). Over the last five years, household sugar consumption has declined by one third, to around 6 ounces per person per week. Purchases of preserves declined by 10 per cent over the same period, with jam and fruit curd consumption showing a lesser fall than that of marmalade.

Table 2.8
Consumption and
expenditure for sugar
and preserves

						per person per week
	Consumption			Expenditure		
	1988	1989	1990	1988	1989	1990
	(ounces)			(pence)		
SUGAR AND PRESERVES:						
Sugar	6.94	6.46	6.04	11.32	11.08	11.10
Honey, preserves, syrup and treacle	1.85	1.76	1.69	6.45	6.57	6.98
Total sugar and preserves	**8.79**	**8.22**	**7.73**	**17.77**	**17.65**	**18.08**

Vegetables and Fruit

Supplies of some fresh vegetables were affected by dry weather and there were marked reductions in the consumption of leafy salads, green beans, onions and leeks and a continued decline for cabbages and Brussels sprouts. Expenditure on fruit averaged nearly £1 per person per week, an increase of 12 per cent over 1989, of which two thirds was on fresh fruit. Consumption of oranges and other citrus fruit was lower than in 1989 but that of bananas was markedly higher. Consumption of more unusual fruits also continued to rise. Higher prices of orange juice, reflecting reduced availability of supplies from North and South America, reversed the recent upward trend in consumption of fruit juice. There was a 15 per cent reduction in purchases of canned fruit since 1989, but an increase for nuts and nut products.

Table 2.9

Consumption and expenditure for vegetables and fruit

per person per week

	Consumption			Expenditure		
	1988	1989	1990	1988	1989	1990
	(ounces) [a]			(pence)		
VEGETABLES:						
Potatoes	36.43	35.59	35.17	22.15	25.18	27.53
Fresh green	10.42	10.23	9.79	19.03	20.69	21.95
Other fresh	16.81	17.13	16.19	41.10	43.13	46.27
Frozen, including vegetable products	6.53	6.70	6.54	17.83	19.09	20.88
Other processed, including vegetable products	12.87	12.35	12.10	45.41	48.29	52.81
Total vegetables	**83.09**	**82.01**	**79.79**	**145.52**	**156.39**	**169.45**
FRUIT:						
Fresh	21.02	21.45	21.33	52.55	56.67	65.06
Fruit juices (fl oz)	7.43	7.52	7.11	15.17	16.06	17.25
Other fruit products	3.48	3.42	3.13	13.74	13.94	14.83
Total fruit	**31.92**	**32.40**	**31.56**	**81.47**	**86.68**	**97.13**

(a) except where otherwise stated.

Bread, Cereals and Cereal Products

Household purchases of bread and cereal products were slightly lower than in 1990 but expenditure was 6 per cent higher. Standard white bread consumption showed less reduction than that of wholemeal loaves. Among the other breads there was little change in consumption of rolls but purchases of Vienna and French breads increased. Purchases of flour declined further, reflecting a continuing trend away from home baking, and consumption of oatmeal and oatmeal products has also fallen. Expenditure on cakes, pastries and breakfast cereals has risen quite sharply over the last two years (Table 2.10).

Table 2.10
Consumption and
expenditure for bread
and cereal products

	Consumption			Expenditure		
per person per week	1988	1989	1990	1988	1989	1990
	(ounces)			(pence)		
BREAD:						
White bread (standard loaves)	15.56	15.32	14.76	27.45	28.29	28.37
Brown bread	3.90	3.66	3.45	8.57	8.43	8.30
Wholemeal bread	4.33	4.11	3.82	9.25	9.19	8.95
Other bread (incl. rolls)	6.48	6.33	6.04	20.48	21.92	22.98
Total bread	**30.28**	**29.43**	**28.09**	**65.75**	**67.82**	**68.59**
OTHER CEREALS AND CEREAL PRODUCTS:						
Flour	3.59	3.28	3.19	3.65	3.63	3.55
Cakes	3.67	3.60	3.65	25.36	26.52	28.98
Pastries	5.28	5.25	5.26	28.25	29.86	31.75
Oatmeal and oat products	0.63	0.55	0.52	2.76	2.19	2.21
Breakfast cereals	4.47	4.45	4.47	22.41	24.32	26.52
Other cereals	6.21	6.77	6.62	32.00	37.72	42.38
Total cereals, including bread	**54.12**	**53.33**	**51.79**	**180.17**	**191.86**	**203.98**

Beverages and Miscellaneous Foods

Consumption of tea declined by a further 6 per cent in 1990 but expenditure
rose by 11 per cent, reflecting in particular higher raw material prices.
Coffee consumption also declined slightly despite lower average prices.
Consumption of soups declined by 12 per cent. Among the other foods,
household purchases of mineral water increased by 6 per cent and
expenditure on ice cream and mousse rose by 10 per cent.

Table 2.11
Consumption and
expenditure for
beverages and
miscellaneous foods

	Consumption			Expenditure		
per person per week	1988	1989	1990	1988	1989	1990
	(ounces)			(pence)		
BEVERAGES:						
Tea	1.65	1.61	1.52	17.39	18.14	20.09
Coffee	0.70	0.65	0.63	22.04	21.91	19.82
Cocoa and drinking chocolate	0.17	0.15	0.16	1.63	1.47	1.69
Branded food drinks	0.15	0.19	0.16	1.27	1.67	1.58
Total beverages	**2.66**	**2.60**	**2.47**	**42.34**	**43.19**	**43.18**
MISCELLANEOUS:						
Soups , canned, dehydrated and powdered	2.93	2.85	2.52	8.00	8.42	7.89
Other foods [a]	na	na	na	35.63	39.78	43.77
Total miscellaneous	**na**	**na**	**na**	**43.63**	**48.20**	**51.66**

(a) including spreads, sauces, icecream, salt and other miscellaneous food items

Soft Drinks

Information obtained about soft drinks is not included in the main analysis of the Survey results[2]. Such items may often be bought without the knowledge of the diary-keeper, resulting in a degree of under-recording, and many more purchases would not be brought into the household supply. Results from the Survey suggest, however, that consumption of soft drinks in the home continues to rise, with low-calorie drinks showing a considerable increase (Table 2.12). Appendix B Table 3 contains further information.

Table 2.12
Purchases and expenditure for soft drinks[a]

	Purchase quantity			Expenditure		
	1988	1989	1990	1988	1989	1990
	(fl oz)			(pence)		
Concentrated	3.60	3.98	4.07	7.06	8.01	8.97
Unconcentrated	10.46	12.17	12.82	12.60	15.47	17.58
Low-calorie	2.74	3.85	4.55	3.22	4.73	6.12
All soft drinks [b]	31.20	35.92	37.72	22.88	28.20	32.67

per person per week

(a) excluding pure fruit juices which are recorded in the survey under fruit products
(b) converted to unconcentrated equivalent

Meals eaten outside the home

The National Food Survey does not currently collect information on snacks and meals bought and eaten outside the home, ie not from the household food supply. It does, however, record some information on the number of such meals (Table 2.13) which enables adjustments to be made to nutritional results in order to compare them with recommended intakes. Numbers of mid-day meals eaten out continued to rise, but in 1990 the total number of meals out declined slightly.

Table 2.13
Number of meals out (not from household supply)

	1988	1989	1990
Mid-day meals out	1.85	1.89	1.93
All meals out	3.69	3.84	3.76

per person per week

---

2 Further information on household expenditure on soft drinks, and information on confectionery, is available from the Family Expenditure Survey, quarterly statistical inquiries of the Business Statistics Office and from trade associations.

This information is broadly consistent with information from the Family Expenditure Survey, which shows that expenditure on meals bought away from the home has been rising quite rapidly.

Table 2.14
Expenditure on household food and on meals bought away from the home

	£ per household per week		
	1979	1984	1989
Household food [a]	21.83	26.07	32.99
Meals bought away from home	3.58	5.36	8.68

(a) including soft drinks, chocolate and sugar confectionery
Source: Family Expenditure Survey

The NFS data show that those living in the South-East tended to have the highest number of meals out. Those living in the Northern regions of England are more likely to eat out for mid-day meals. The average number of meals out was markedly dependent on household composition, and especially on the number of children in the household. Those in larger households and households with several children were least likely to eat out (Appendix B Table 4).

Information on the source of mid-day meals for children aged 5 - 14 has been collected continuously since 1972. Analysis of these data show that the number of packed lunches has quadrupled over this period, while there has been a marked decline in meals at home and, to a lesser extent, school lunches. Numbers of other meals out, although small, have tripled since 1972.

Figure 2.15
Average number of mid-day meals per week per child aged 5-14 years

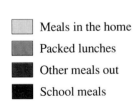

Meals in the home
Packed lunches
Other meals out
School meals

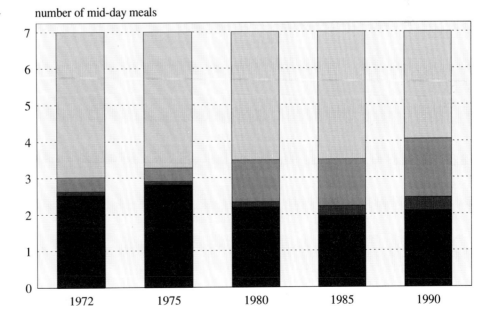

11

These results need to be interpreted with some care. They are averages which relate to the whole year, whereas school lunches will be available on average for about half the days in the year and most mid-day meals from the household supply will relate to holidays and weekends.

Within these data, there are again considerable variations across different groups of people. For example, children in single-parent families (or those being catered for by one adult) had the highest proportion of school meals and the lowest proportion of packed lunches. Children in households where the head of household was in income group A or B were more likely to take packed lunches than have school meals, as were children in the South of England. Children in Scotland were least likely to have mid-day meals away from home (Appendix B Table 5).

Regional Comparisons

The Survey is designed to be representative of Great Britain as a whole, but practical considerations limit the number of areas which can be included from each region in any one year (see Appendix A for the structure of the Survey). For this reason, comparisons between regions must be interpreted with caution.

Total weekly expenditure on household food ranged from £11.09 per person per week in the North West region to £12.91 in the South East and East Anglia region (Table 2.16). Within this, there is also considerable regional variation in consumption of different foods. Consumption of milk and cream, for example, was highest in the East Midlands. Consumption of meat and meat products was highest in the West Midlands, although expenditure on meats was greatest in Scotland. Households in the Northern regions consumed most eggs, and fish consumption was highest in Yorkshire and Humberside. Consumption of cereal products was highest in Scotland and lowest in the South East and East Anglia. Eggs, cheese and fruit showed a particularly high regional variation in levels, whereas meat and meat products showed least variation.

Table 2.16

Expenditure and consumption for selected foods by region, 1990

per person per week

		Regions of England						England	Wales	Scotland	All households
	North	Yorkshire and Humberside	North West	East Midlands	West Midlands	South West	South East/East Anglia				
EXPENDITURE						pence					
Milk and cream	117.8	130.80	121.58	140.05	116.91	127.46	135.33	129.14	119.32	118.18	127.69
Cheese	34.49	37.89	34.61	42.42	36.75	50.49	46.23	41.83	33.43	42.97	41.43
Meat and meat products	320.95	327.60	321.36	323.95	330.33	325.77	346.33	333.35	339.16	375.24	337.24
Fish	67.54	79.16	58.99	61.31	57.75	60.12	73.34	67.51	63.55	58.70	66.62
Eggs	23.52	20.20	19.12	18.28	16.55	19.84	19.11	19.21	19.60	22.23	19.49
Fats and oils	34.91	34.05	32.32	36.28	34.65	40.36	35.75	35.36	41.73	39.69	36.11
Sugar and preserves	21.04	16.67	17.16	15.82	17.46	20.33	17.62	17.82	19.07	19.76	18.08
Fruit	84.04	86.13	77.71	91.06	71.08	99.57	122.48	98.93	82.85	88.44	97.08
Vegetables	158.97	167.26	155.31	172.98	162.95	170.84	184.15	171.79	160.51	155.89	169.76
Cereals (incl. bread)	200.53	202.40	190.01	194.25	189.36	205.67	210.81	201.98	186.91	235.84	203.98
Beverages	45.42	45.89	39.68	40.42	41.91	46.42	42.23	42.78	43.26	47.02	43.18
Other foods	48.75	48.03	41.90	49.71	43.21	56.76	58.25	51.56	45.54	56.74	51.66
Total	**£11.57**	**£11.99**	**£11.04**	**£11.86**	**£11.19**	**£12.25**	**£12.91**	**£12.11**	**£11.53**	**£12.60**	**£12.12**
CONSUMPTION						ounces [a]					
Milk and cream (pt or eq pt)	3.67	4.01	3.68	4.18	3.61	4.03	3.77	3.81	3.83	3.80	3.82
Cheese	3.41	3.76	3.50	4.31	3.66	4.81	4.28	4.03	3.38	4.11	4.00
Meat and meat products	35.63	34.44	33.05	33.62	36.02	34.33	33.21	33.95	35.92	34.48	34.11
Fish	5.29	5.96	4.67	4.77	4.51	4.69	5.31	5.09	5.42	4.70	5.08
Eggs (no)	2.89	2.38	2.28	2.19	1.90	2.30	1.98	2.17	2.14	2.61	2.20
Fats and oils	9.29	8.98	7.83	9.12	9.02	10.11	8.75	8.87	10.42	9.33	9.00
Sugar and preserves	9.17	7.32	7.49	7.02	8.36	8.21	7.12	7.58	8.49	8.57	7.73
Fruit	29.25	30.26	25.55	31.00	24.19	33.57	37.74	32.16	26.80	28.96	31.56
Vegetables	83.89	80.67	80.10	80.14	81.26	88.31	74.04	79.04	87.23	81.50	79.79
Cereals (incl. bread)	56.79	53.20	48.08	50.79	53.35	52.36	49.55	51.06	52.75	58.51	51.79
Beverages	2.50	2.60	2.31	2.41	2.48	2.59	2.42	2.45	2.67	2.46	2.47

(a) except where otherwise stated

Consumption of fish varied considerably by region (Figure 2.17), with Yorkshire and Humberside having the highest level overall. Within this, consumption of fresh fish was lowest in the West Midlands and highest in Scotland which benefits from a long coastline and good salmon industry. Prepared fish and fish products were consumed most in Yorkshire and Humberside. The East Midlands and Scotland had the lowest consumption of frozen fish and fish products, whilst the highest consumption was in households in Wales.

Figure 2.17
Consumption of fish
by region, 1990

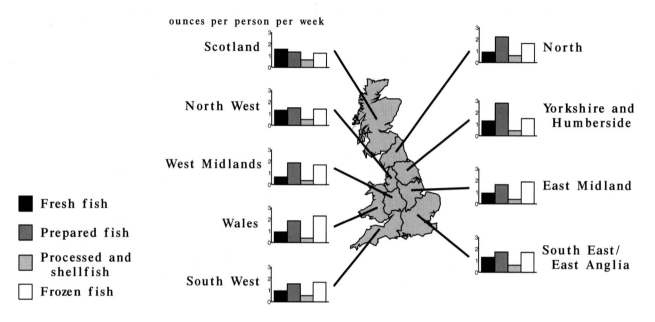

Consumption of cereals and cereal products, excluding bread, was lowest overall in households in Wales, the North West and West Midlands (Figure 2.18). Within this, consumption of flour was nearly three times as high in the North and in Yorkshire and Humberside as in the North West. The North Western households consumed a higher proportion of purchased cakes and biscuits, although in all regions this represented more than a third of the total cereals illustrated. Scotland showed the highest consumption of 'other' cereals, including oatmeal and convenience savouries.

Figure 2.18
Consumption of cereals
by region, 1990

Flour
Cakes
Biscuits
Breakfast cereals
Other cereals

Fresh fruit consumption shows less regional variation, although it continues, on average, to be lower in the north than in the south of the country (Figure 2.19). The South East and East Anglia had the highest total consumption of fresh fruit, particularly of apples and bananas. Consumption of oranges was high in the North and low in the Midlands. Consumption of bananas accounted for around one fifth of the total fresh fruit consumption in all regions.

Figure 2.19
Consumption of fresh
fruit by region, 1990

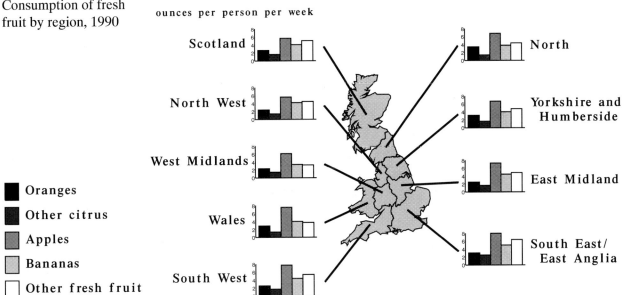

Oranges
Other citrus
Apples
Bananas
Other fresh fruit

Income Group Comparisons

The distribution of households by income group[3] will always differ slightly from the target distribution and from that achieved in previous years. As a result, average values for food consumption and expenditure by income group are not fully comparable with those for earlier years. This classification problem does not affect the 'national' averages for the sample as a whole. Table 2.20 shows expenditure and consumption by income group for the 1990 sample.

Table 2.20
Expenditure and consumption for selected foods by income group, 1990

per person per week

	INCOME GROUP [a]						
	Gross weekly income of head of household						
	Households with one or more earners				Households without an earner		OAP
	A	B	C	D	E1	E2	
EXPENDITURE	pence						
Milk and cream	136.16	127.64	123.01	118.59	160.95	121.34	135.16
Cheese	53.97	43.08	37.92	32.43	55.81	36.10	35.22
Meat and meat products	354.15	344.13	335.61	299.33	394.94	311.81	318.02
Fish	77.38	63.71	56.93	56.33	120.20	70.43	81.36
Eggs	18.25	16.55	19.56	21.93	26.36	22.73	28.05
Fats and oils	35.07	33.84	34.44	32.32	45.51	40.82	49.96
Sugar and preserves	14.75	14.90	16.67	19.94	30.11	22.87	33.49
Fruit	142.60	101.97	78.94	61.39	160.38	83.59	90.76
Vegetables	187.53	179.25	162.11	153.01	180.75	160.09	135.66
Cereals (incl. bread)	211.33	211.44	196.46	185.59	224.06	191.91	202.46
Beverages	40.01	39.02	40.68	42.79	63.72	51.74	60.26
Other foods	63.25	54.40	47.62	42.93	64.40	46.08	42.92
Total	**£13.34**	**£12.30**	**£11.50**	**£10.67**	**£15.27**	**£11.60**	**£12.13**
CONSUMPTION	ounces [b]						
Milk and cream (pt or eq pt)	3.68	3.70	3.74	3.87	4.72	4.00	4.31
Cheese	4.78	4.17	3.75	3.46	5.05	3.53	3.50
Meat and meat products	31.29	34.41	34.55	33.80	38.36	34.10	33.31
Fish	4.87	4.82	4.54	4.67	8.80	5.69	6.65
Eggs (no)	1.90	1.85	2.27	2.61	2.78	2.65	3.13
Fats and oils	7.60	8.41	8.77	8.81	10.33	10.82	12.34
Sugar and preserves	5.44	6.14	7.64	9.22	11.77	10.18	14.08
Fruit	42.55	32.90	26.31	20.60	53.45	28.50	31.00
Vegetables	67.92	75.55	81.54	82.77	95.41	93.41	82.82
Cereals (incl. bread)	45.41	50.43	52.11	53.79	58.04	55.41	58.00
Beverages	2.17	2.09	2.31	2.65	3.67	3.23	3.90
Other foods	15.38	12.26	10.73	10.12	15.29	10.41	10.72

(a) definition : A £475 and over, B £250 and under £475, C £125 and under £250, D less than £125, E1 £125 or more, E2 less than £125

(b) except where otherwise stated

---

3 Respondents are often reluctant or unable to give precise details of the income of the head of household or, where appropriate, the principal earner. In such cases they are asked to state the income group in which it lies. Details of the sample of households in each income group for 1990 are given in Appendix A.

For those households with at least one earner, average expenditure on household food increased with the income of the head of household. However, the highest average expenditure occurred in the non-earner group E1, and averages for E2 and pensioner households were also above those for earning households at comparable or even higher income levels. This reflects the fact that the non-earner groups contain fewer children and household members eat out less than in the earner groups. So, although there are a number of factors which affect the level of household food expenditure, households with higher incomes tend to spend most on food. This relationship does not hold for all food groups within the total. For example, high income families tend to spend less on basic foods such as bread, flour, eggs, potatoes, tea and sugar. Appendix B Tables 6 and 7 give further details of consumption and expenditure by income group of the head of household.

The following figures illustrate the variation in consumption and expenditure by income group for selected foods. Total consumption of fats in households with an earner reduces as income increases, although expenditure on fats tends to increase slightly (Figure 2.21). Pensioner households have the highest consumption and expenditure for fats, followed by the non-earner groups E1 and E2. In particular, they consume more butter and margarine; the consumption of vegetable and salad oils and low or reduced fat spreads is similar in higher earning groups.

Figure 2.21
Consumption and
expenditure for fats
according to income
group, 1990

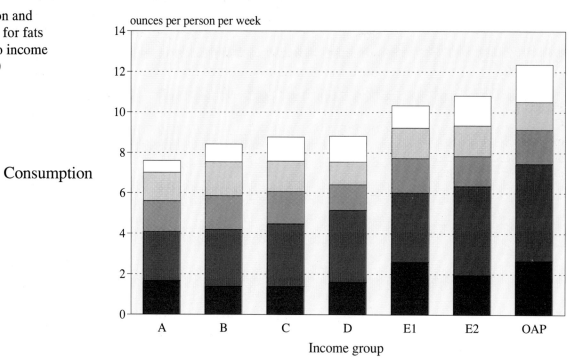

Consumption

All other fats
Vegetable and salad oils
Low fat and dairy spreads
Margarine
Butter

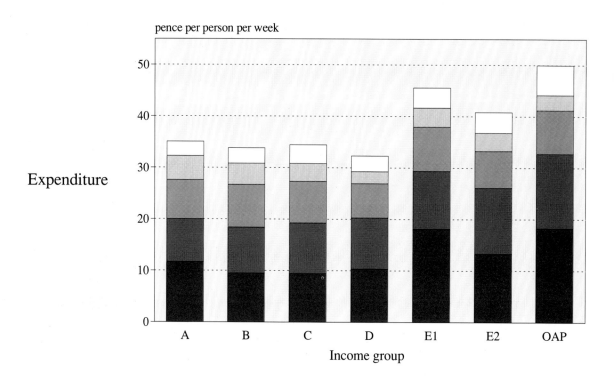

Expenditure

Consumption and expenditure figures for sugar show a very marked reduction with increasing income, and the highest consumption of sugar and preserves is in non-earning households (Figure 2.22). This, together with similar trends observed for fats, flour and eggs, implies that it is the households with no earners which do most baking.

Figure 2.22
Consumption and expenditure for sugar and preserves according to inome group, 1990

Consumption

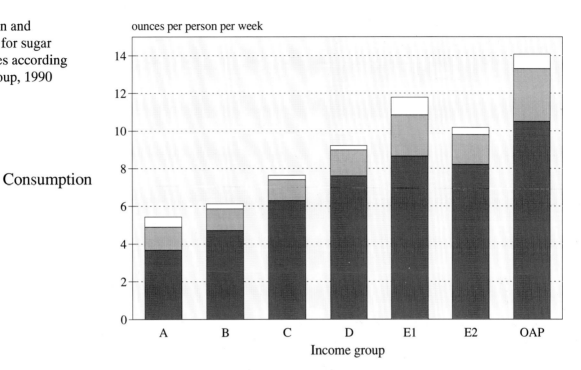

Syrup, treacle and honey
Jams and marmalade
Sugar

Expenditure

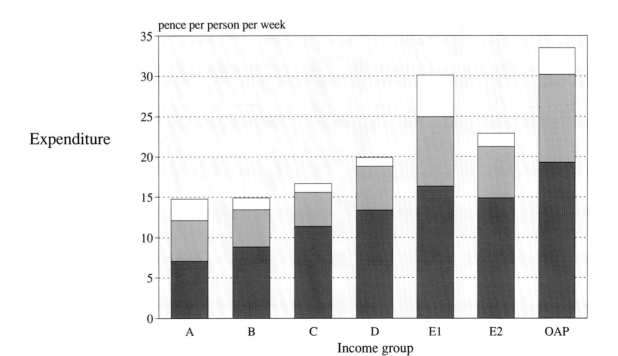

Consumption of fresh fruit and, even more markedly, fruit juices increases significantly with income (Figure 2.23). Although consumption of other fruit and fruit products also increases with income, this is highest in the non-earning households, particularly those with a higher income (group E1).

Figure 2.23
Consumption and expenditure for fruit according to income group, 1990

Consumption

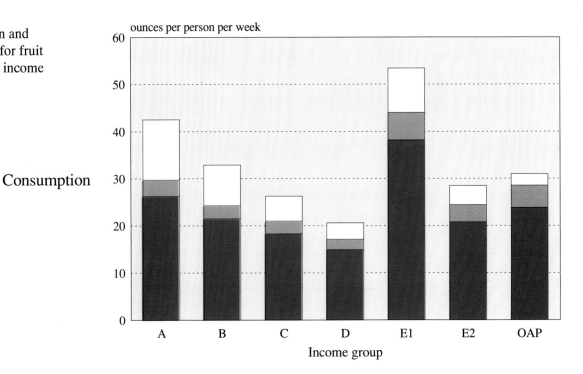

☐ Fruit juice
▨ Other fruit and fruit products
■ Fresh fruit

Expenditure

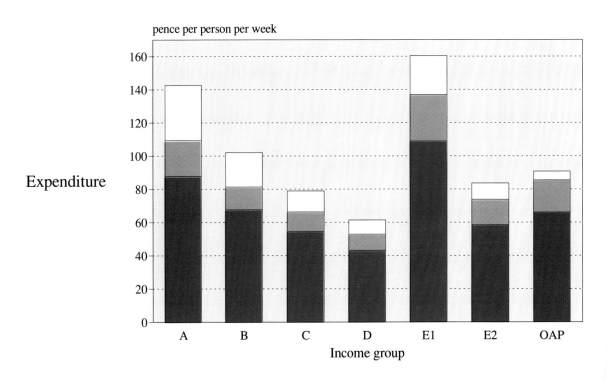

Household Composition Comparisons

Perhaps the most important factor affecting household food consumption and expenditure is the number of children and adults in the household. Table 2.24 illustrates how total expenditure on household food, and consumption of selected foods, varies by household composition. More detailed information is given in Appendix B Table 8.

Table 2.24
Consumption of selected foods by household composition, 1990

ounces per person per week [a]

	Households with										
No of adults	1		2					3	3 or more		4 or more
No of children	0	1 or more	0	1	2	3	4 or more	0	1 or 2	3 or more	0
Milk and cream (pt or eq. pt)	4.55	3.82	4.07	3.94	3.58	3.40	3.48	3.85	3.49	3.25	3.60
Cheese	4.64	2.90	4.78	3.70	3.65	2.94	2.87	4.37	3.85	2.23	4.45
Carcase meat	10.16	7.42	14.26	11.04	8.04	9.21	9.47	14.29	10.74	7.87	12.03
Other meat and meat products	24.95	19.27	26.22	23.71	19.59	17.41	17.96	27.22	22.41	16.57	25.69
Fish	6.84	2.74	7.13	4.61	3.66	3.09	3.04	5.59	4.24	4.03	5.19
Eggs (no)	3.00	1.82	2.71	2.02	1.62	1.75	1.79	2.58	1.94	1.73	2.12
Fats	10.76	7.12	11.40	7.98	6.94	6.56	7.07	9.78	7.94	8.15	11.01
Sugar and preserves	11.94	5.86	9.93	6.83	5.49	5.66	6.68	8.01	6.16	5.40	8.30
Potatoes	31.32	33.86	42.43	32.92	26.65	31.34	35.59	42.85	33.45	30.40	39.23
Fresh green vegetables	12.14	5.88	13.82	8.87	6.40	5.88	4.91	12.60	8.56	6.20	10.39
Other fresh vegetables	19.25	9.78	21.14	16.26	12.27	10.91	9.52	18.58	15.76	11.91	15.95
Processed vegetables	17.96	18.71	19.44	20.42	18.09	17.46	18.26	19.07	17.51	16.25	19.22
Fresh fruit	30.13	12.99	27.70	19.61	17.18	14.74	16.34	22.91	17.20	11.54	20.60
Other fruit and fruit products	11.86	6.31	12.11	11.26	10.54	7.66	4.33	9.18	8.78	7.72	10.03
Bread	33.16	26.72	30.64	27.19	24.60	23.29	23.49	32.19	26.69	20.60	31.54
Other cereals	27.67	21.58	25.68	22.32	23.17	20.79	27.63	22.92	21.08	23.20	22.36
Tea	2.47	1.14	2.09	1.30	1.00	1.10	0.89	1.61	1.15	1.13	1.43
Coffee	0.83	0.42	0.83	0.60	0.48	0.45	0.40	0.69	0.51	0.33	0.74
Cocoa and drinking chocolate	0.17	0.22	0.13	0.20	0.18	0.13	0.33	0.17	0.11	0.14	0.15
Branded food drinks	0.38	0.04	0.29	0.09	0.06	0.03	...	0.14	0.09	...	0.17
Other foods	13.19	10.97	13.90	12.78	11.09	9.72	9.09	10.97	10.40	9.51	10.95
Total expenditure	**£14.41**	**£9.23**	**£14.52**	**£12.39**	**£10.35**	**£8.97**	**£8.69**	**£13.37**	**£11.04**	**£8.47**	**£12.62**

(a) except where otherwise stated

There are clearly some economies of scale in food purchases. Larger sizes of items often represent better value for money, and food spoilage and waste may be less of a problem in larger households. Figure 2.25 shows that per capita expenditure decreased for all-adult households with more than two members. This is particularly noticeable for milk and dairy products and fruit and vegetables.

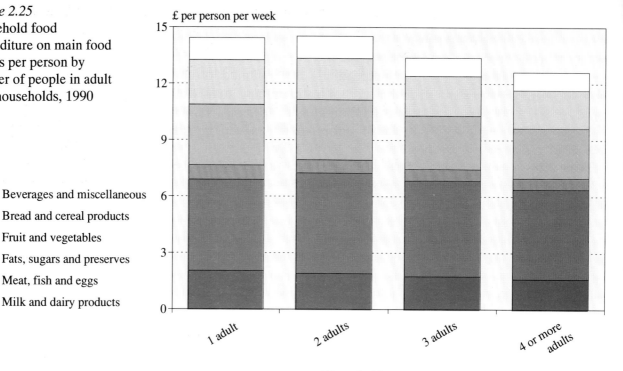

Figure 2.25
Household food expenditure on main food groups per person by number of people in adult only households, 1990

Beverages and miscellaneous

Bread and cereal products

Fruit and vegetables

Fats, sugars and preserves

Meat, fish and eggs

Milk and dairy products

The food requirements of children are on average less than for adults so, as Figure 2.26 shows, there is an even more marked reduction in per capita expenditure for two-adult households as the number of children increases. Unlike adult only households, the most pronounced reduction as an extra person is added is for meat, fish and eggs, with a strong decline also for fruit and vegetable expenditure.

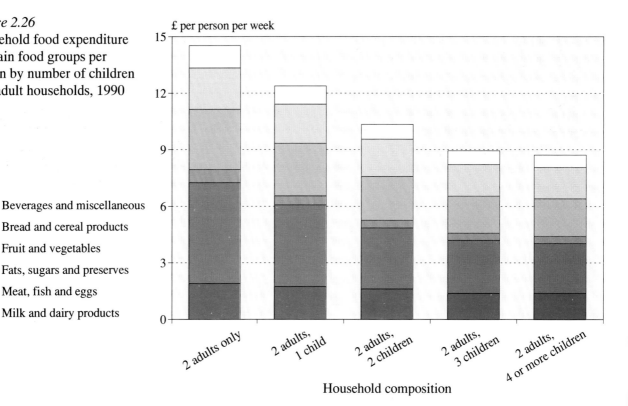

Figure 2.26
Household food expenditure on main food groups per person by number of children in 2-adult households, 1990

Beverages and miscellaneous

Bread and cereal products

Fruit and vegetables

Fats, sugars and preserves

Meat, fish and eggs

Milk and dairy products

This general pattern of a decline in expenditure per head as numbers of adults, or of children, in the household increases is illustrated for fresh fruit (Figure 2.27) and for sugar and preserves (Figure 2.28). Expenditure on apples is least affected by household composition, whereas 'other' fresh fruit, which includes soft fruit, stone fruit and exotics, shows greatest variation. Expenditure on brown and wholemeal bread shows the same decline with higher numbers of adults or children, but expenditure on white bread is more consistent, although it is high for three and four-adult families (Figure 2.29). Expenditure on other bread tends to decline only with increasing numbers of children and not increasing numbers of adults.

Figure 2.27
Expenditure on fresh fruit by household composition,1990

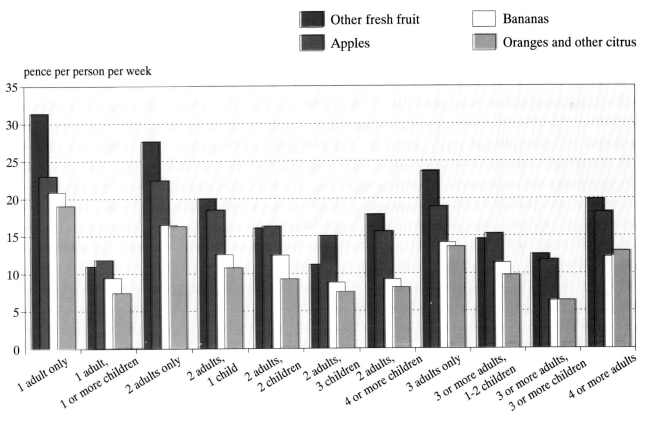

Figure 2.28
Expenditure on sugar and preserves by household composition, 1990

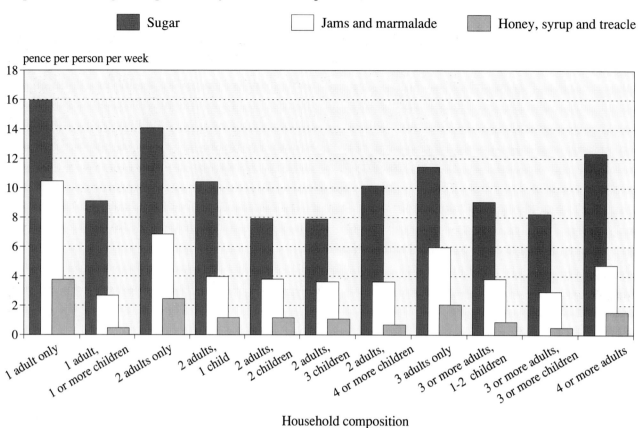

Household composition

Figure 2.29
Expenditure on bread by household composition, 1990

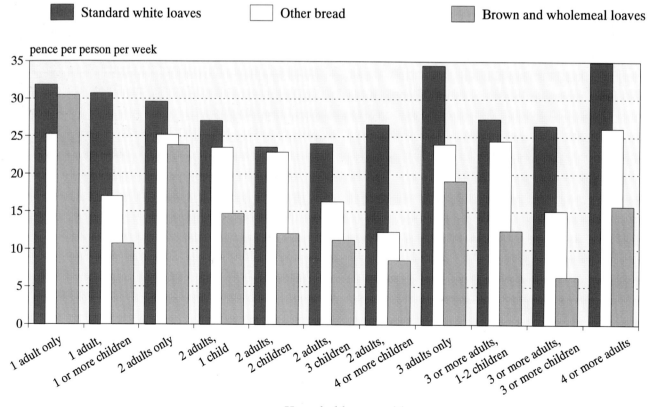

Household composition

24

Household Composition Groups within Income Groups

In general household composition has a greater influence on average per capita expenditure than income group, but the effect is not always the same in each income group (Figure 2.30). For example the reduction in average expenditure as an extra child is added to a household is greater in groups D and E2 than in income group C. One adult families with children showed the greatest variation in expenditure between households of different income groups, although there were insufficient households of this composition in group A to observe the full effect. The highest expenditure, £16.82 per week, occurred in all-adult households in income group A, and the lowest, £6.69, in households with 2 adults and 4 or more children in income groups D and E2.

Figure 2.30
Total household food expenditure per head by certain household composition groups within income groups, 1990

Income group

A
B
C
D+E2

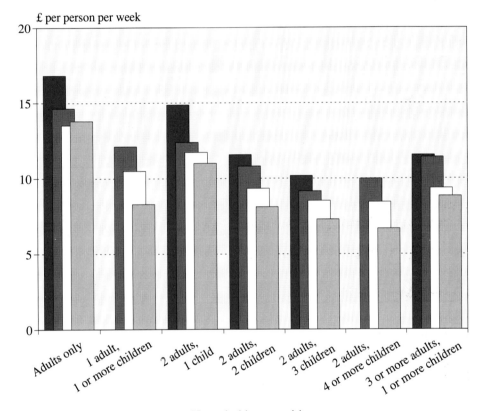

Figure 2.31 shows how expenditure on selected foods varies with household composition and income group. Expenditure on carcase meat varies considerably by household composition, but the relationship with income group is less clear-cut. For fish, household composition has a marked effect with expenditure falling greatly as the number of children increases, especially in income groups D and E2. Households dominated by adults in income groups D and E2 spend more on fish than equivalent families in groups B or C. Household composition is less a factor for cheese, but the relationship with income group is pronounced. Appendix B Table 9 gives details of average consumption of selected foods for households classified by income group and household composition.

Figure 2.31
Expenditure on selected foods by certain household composition groups within income groups, 1990

Carcase meat

Income group

A
B
C
D+E2

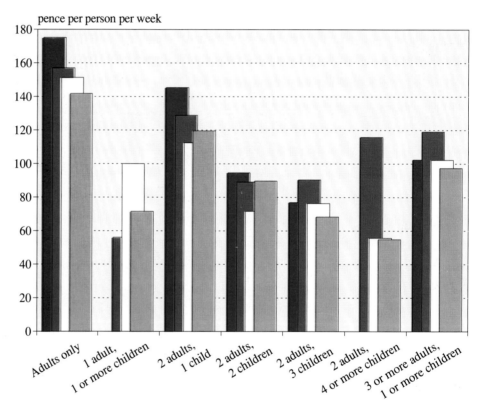

Household composition

Figure 2.31 continued

Fish

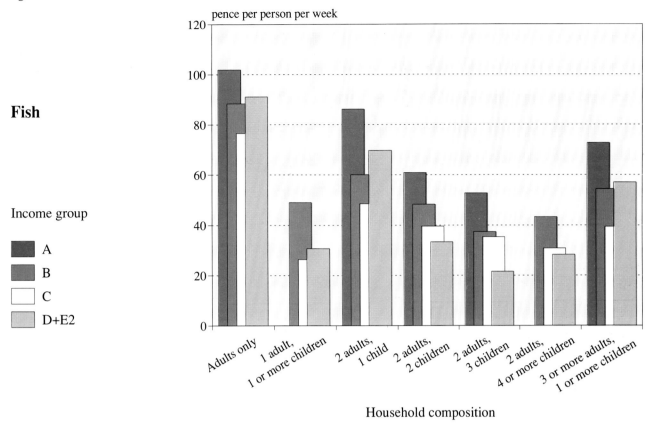

Cheese

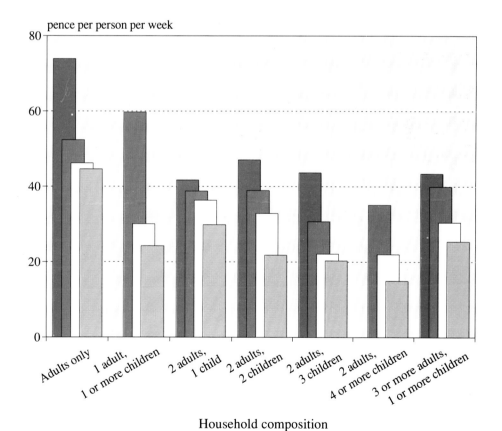

Section 3

Nutritional Results

National Averages

In this section of the Report, the nutritional value of the food brought into homes throughout Britain in 1990 is summarised and compared with the values recorded in 1988 and 1989. More detailed results for 1990, including the contributions made by selected foods to average nutrient intakes, are shown in Appendix B Tables 10-14. As in every year since 1979, the values for each group of the population have been compared with the recommended daily amounts (RDA) of energy and nutrients published by the Department of Health and Social Security in 1979[1]. In addition, some comparisons have also been made with the reference nutrient intakes (RNI) and, for energy, with the esimated average requirements from the new report on dietary reference values for food energy and nutrients for the United Kingdom which was published by the Department of Health[2] while the present report was in preparation.

Energy

The average household diet in 1990 provided 1,872 kcal per person per day in 1990, compared with 1,941 kcal in 1989 and 1,998 kcal in 1988. The amount of food brought into the home has declined steadily since 1970, partly because less food is needed by an increasingly sedentary population and partly because food eaten outside the home and alcoholic drinks and confectionary, which are not yet recorded by the Survey, make an increasingly important contribution to total energy needs (Table 3.1).

Table 3.1

Energy value of household food, drinks and confectionary

	1970	1988	1989	kcal per person per day 1990
Household food	2597	1988	1941	1872
Soft drinks brought into the home	17 [a]	30	34	36
Alcoholic drinks [b]	129	159	159	158
Sugar and chocolate confectionery [b]	135	150	149	154
TOTAL (to the nearest 10 kcal)	2860	2340	2280	2220
Number of meals eaten outside the home	2.69 [c]	3.69	3.84	3.76

(a) 1975   (b) Derived from supply figures   (c) 1973

1 Department of Health and Social Security. *Recommended Daily Amounts of Food Energy and Nutrients for Groups of People in the United Kingdom.* Report on Health and Social Subjects No.15, HMSO, 1979.

2 Department of Health. *Dietary Reference Values for Food Energy and Nutrients for the United Kingdom.* Report on Health and Social Subjects No.41, HMSO, 1991.

The energy value of the household food supply met 86 per cent of the RDA, after an allowance for meals eaten out and a conventional deduction of 10 per cent for wastage of edible food in the home, but 90 per cent of the new dietary reference value. A shortage of food energy is not, however, a problem in Britain. The Dietary and Nutritional Survey of British Adults[3] showed an increase in obesity to the point that half of the male participants and one third of the female participants in that Survey could be classified as overweight.

The relative contributions made by the main groups of foods to selected nutrients is shown in Appendix B Table 14. There were declines in the amount of energy provided by all the main food groups, although their relative contributions were little different from those in 1989. Compared with 1970, however, smaller contributions were made by milk (6.5 compared with 9.9 per cent), meats (15.7 compared with 16.5 per cent) and sugar and preserves (6.1 compared with 11.5 per cent). On the other hand, greater contributions were made by cheese (3.3 compared with 2.2 per cent), vegetables (9.9 compared with 7.6 per cent) and cereal products (31.5 compared with 29.4 per cent).

Fats, carbohydrates and fibre

The energy value of food is primarily derived from its fat, protein and carbohydrate (sugars and starch) content. The new dietary reference values set out changes to the balance of the UK diet which should result in improvements in health. In Table 3.2 the dietary reference values for fat, saturated fatty acids and carbohydrate are compared with the proportions of energy derived from these in the Survey in 1990 and in 1970.

Table 3.2

Proportions of household food energy derived from fat, protein and carbohydrate

	NFS 1970	NFS 1990	Dietary reference values
Fat	41.8	41.6	35
Saturated fatty acids	19.9 [a]	16.6	11
Carbohydrate	46.5	45.9	50

(a) 1969

Although the amount of fat in the household diet has fallen steadily from 121g per person per day in 1970 to 86g in 1990, the amount of energy has also fallen with that decline and a decrease in carbohydrate (especially sugar). The proportion of energy from fat has therefore changed little since 1970, and has not been as low as 35 per cent since 1947 when the British diet was very austere.

---

3 J Gregory, K Foster, H Tyler and M Wiseman. *The Dietary and Nutritional Survey of British Adults*, HMSO, 1990.

The dietary reference value for carbohydrate has been subdivided into 11 per cent from non-milk extrinsic sugars and 39 per cent from other sugars and starch. The household diet was estimated to have provided 57g non-milk extrinsic sugars in 1990, derived mainly from table sugar, fruit juices, honey and the sugars added during the manufacture of foods. This is equivalent to 11.4 per cent of the household food energy, but it would have been supplemented by the sugars in alcoholic drinks and confectionary which are not recorded in the Survey and which are all extrinsic.

The dietary reference value for fibre is 18g non-starch polysaccharide per day except for young children. Although the household diet provided only 12.1g in 1990, compared with 12.4g in 1989 and 13.0g in 1986, in part because of the decline in the consumption of wholemeal bread since 1986, the concentration of non-starch polysaccharides in the diet has risen from 6.3g per 1000 kcal in 1986 to 6.5g per 1000 kcal in 1990.

Minerals and vitamins

The amounts of two minerals and six vitamins have been evaluated in the National Food Survey almost since it began in 1940. After an allowance for meals eaten out and a deduction of 10 per cent of the totals for wastage, these have been compared with recommended intakes of the nutrients. Since 1979, the recommendations were those issued by the Department of Health and Social Security in that year, and Appendix B Tables 10-13 continue to compare the intakes in different categories of household with these recommendations. In addition, Table 3.3 shows how the national average household diet compares with the new Reference Nutrient Intakes (the highest of the three reference values for each nutrient).

Table 3.3

Household intakes in 1990 of minerals and vitamins expressed as percentages of recommended amounts or reference intakes

	% of 1979 RDAs	% of 1991 RNIs
Calcium	153	121
Magnesium	-	84
Iron	99	98
Zinc	-	100
Copper	-	104
Vitamin A	160	188
Thiamin	142	157
Riboflavin	119	143
Niacin	164	183
Vitamin B_6	-	133
Vitamin B_{12}	-	369
Folate	-	131
Vitamin C	185	139

Regional, Household Composition and Income Group Differences

The nutritional value of the diets in households in different regions and with different household composition and incomes are shown in Appendix B Tables 11-13. As in previous years, the variations were smaller than the variations in dietary patterns because foods of broadly similar nutritional value, such as beef and lamb or butter and margarine, tend to be substituted for one another. However, because consumption of most of the main sources of vitamin C continues to be lower in Scotland and the North of England than elsewhere, as well as in larger and poorer families, intakes of vitamin C show a greater variation than intakes of the other nutrients that have been evaluated in detail.

Table 3.4 compares the variations in vitamin C with those of fat in different regions and income groups, and in families with two adults and different numbers of children. Vitamin C intakes ranged from 40 mg to 60 mg per day, with intakes (as in previous years) highest in the South of England, in richer households and most especially in smaller families. In contrast, the proportion of energy derived from fat lay only between 40 and 42 per cent in all categories of household apart from the very largest families, and the ratio of the polyunsaturated to saturated fatty acids was never lower than 0.38 nor higher than 0.42. What variations there were in the proportion and type of fat were not closely related to the variations that occur within Britain in heart disease.

Table 3.4
Selected nutritional results by region, income group and in households with 2 adults and different numbers of children in 1990

				Regions of England						
	Scotland	Wales	England	North	Yorkshire/ Humberside	North West	East Midlands	West Midlands	South West	SouthEast/ East Anglia
P/S ratio	0.39	0.40	0.40	0.39	0.40	0.38	0.42	0.40	0.40	0.41
% energy from fat	40.5	42.1	41.6	40.3	41.3	41.1	42.3	41.3	42.2	42.0
Vitamin C (mg)	50	47	53	53	52	45	52	47	57	57

	Numbers of children					Income group							
	0	1	2	3	4 or more	A	B	C	D	E1	E2	OAP	All
P/S ratio	0.40	0.41	0.40	0.40	0.41	0.40	0.41	0.40	0.38	0.37	0.40	0.38	0.40
% energy from fat	42.4	41.7	40.6	40.3	38.5	42.1	42.0	41.3	40.8	40.3	41.3	41.4	41.5
Vitamin C (mg)	62	55	46	42	40	62	53	48	44	72	51	48	52

Section 4

Analysis of Historical Data from the Survey

Background

The Survey results have been documented in Annual Reports since 1950, with two earlier reports covering the first ten years. These volumes form a unique historical record of the Survey, and contain a wealth of information about household food consumption and expenditure in Britain over the last fifty years. This section provides illustrations of the changes which have taken place over this time. Tables of historical data are contained in Appendix C.

The NFS was initiated in 1940 by the then Ministry of Food and was intended to provide an independent check on the population's diet during the Second World War. It was then continued in the same form until 1949 in order to provide information on the effects of post-war food policies such as de-rationing. Throughout this period, the Survey covered mainly working-class households where it was expected that the effects of any food shortages would be most noticeable. A representative national sample of all households was not employed until 1950, and from 1952 onwards, the Survey was continuous. The Annual Reports contained detailed tables of both consumption and expenditure with sub analyses by income group, household composition and, from 1955, region. Many of the illustrations which follow take 1952 as a starting point, although earlier data are used where it is reasonable to do so. Inevitably, definitions and classifications have changed from time to time and major differences are pointed out. Such factors need to be taken into account when interpreting the tables and charts.

Trends in Household Food Consumption and Expenditure

Expenditure on household food has risen steadily over the last 50 years (Table 4.1) with food prices moving, for the most part, in line with inflation. During the war and in the early years after the war, food obtained from gardens and allotments accounted for nearly 10 per cent of the value of household food. Its contribution to household food supplies has declined but remains significant.

Table 4.1

Household food expenditure
and total value of food
obtained for consumption

£ per person per week

Year	Expenditure on food	Value of free food	Value of consumption
1940	0.48[a,b]	na	na
1945	0.55[a]	na	na
1950	0.74	0.07	0.81
1955	1.28	0.05	1.33
1960	1.48	0.04	1.53
1965	1.72	0.04	1.77
1970	2.11	0.05	2.16
1975	3.77	0.09	3.87
1980	7.21	0.16	7.38
1985	9.17	0.20	9.37
1990	12.12	0.23	12.35

(a) Urban working-class households only
(b) July 1940

Expenditure on household food has risen slowly relative to income and now represents only 12 per cent of total household expenditure compared with 30 per cent in 1940 (Figure 4.2).

Figure 4.2
Expenditure on household food as a percentage of total household expenditure

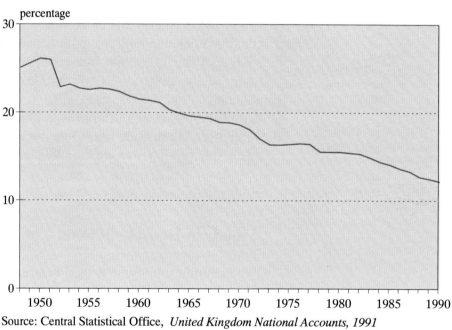

Source: Central Statistical Office, *United Kingdom National Accounts, 1991*

Over the last 50 years, the proportions of household food expenditure represented by the main food groups have remained remarkably stable (Figure 4.3). There has been some reduction in the share of sugar and preserves reflecting the decline in home baking and preserving. Also, since 1980, the proportions spent on fruit and vegetables have increased while those on meat, fish and eggs have marginally declined. There have, however, been significant changes within food groups and some of these are described below.

Figure 4.3
Percentage of household
food expenditure on main
food groups

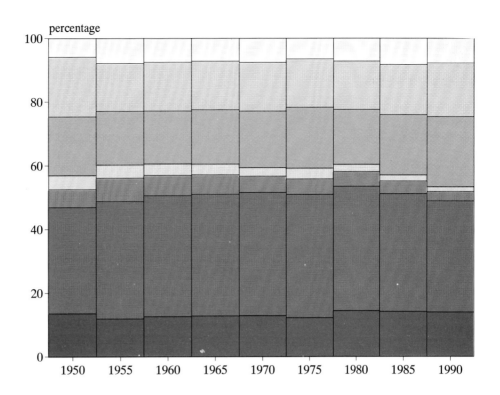

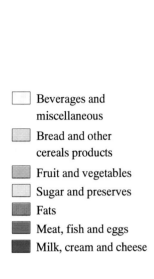

- Beverages and
  miscellaneous
- Bread and other
  cereals products
- Fruit and vegetables
- Sugar and preserves
- Fats
- Meat, fish and eggs
- Milk, cream and cheese

Bread

Two fundamental objectives of wartime food policy were to ensure
an adequate supply of bread, and to do so without rationing. This
was achieved partly by increased home production of wheat, and partly
by raising the extraction rate for flour. The sale of white bread was
banned early in 1942 and consumption of National Bread, a
'high extraction' (or brown bread) product which was price controlled
and subsidised, became the norm. White bread did not become available
again until 1953 and, by the time de-control took place in 1956, it
had virtually replaced brown bread in popularity (Figure 4.4). Bread

Figure 4.4
Consumption of bread

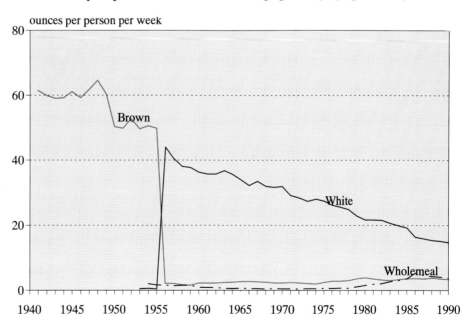

consumption has declined almost throughout the entire post war period as lifestyles have changed and energy requirements have reduced. However, over the last decade, there has been a marked switch towards wholemeal bread with its 'healthy' image.

Fats

Butter and other fats, with the exception of suet and dripping, were rationed during the war. Butter consumption subsequently rose rapidly when supplies improved, but with a sharp dip in 1952 reflecting balance of payments difficulties. For about thirty years from 1955, relative prices had a major influence on consumption levels for butter and margarine often resulting in a rise in consumption of one being offset by reduced consumption of the other. More recently, butter consumption has declined to below wartime levels and margarine consumption has also declined being replaced in part by the growth in demand for low fat and reduced fat spreads.

Figure 4.5
Consumption of fats

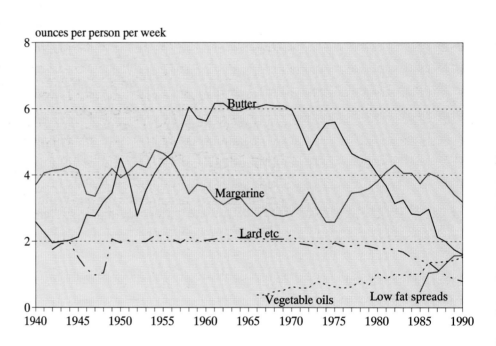

Milk and milk products

Consumption of milk and milk products was relatively stable in the post war years. However, more recent concern over fat in the diet and cholesterol levels has had a major impact on consumption of dairy products. In particular, purchases of wholemilk have declined rapidly and are now less than half the level of 1975. This decline has been partly offset by a switch to low fat milks (Figure 4.6).

Figure 4.6
Consumption of milk
and milk products

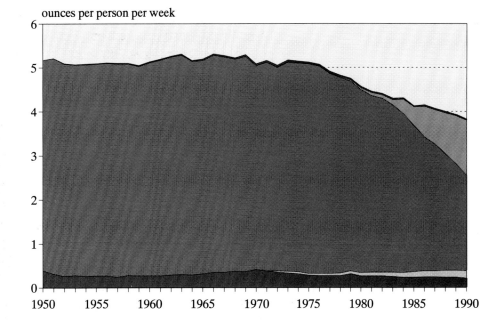

ounces per person per week

Cream
Total skimmed milk
Wholemilk
Yoghurt
Other milk

Meat

With imports curtailed and farm production diverted to milk and arable crops, meat rationing was introduced in 1940. Weekly per capita consumption of carcase meat fell from around 40 ounces to less than 20 ounces in 1940 and, by 1941, to only some 13-14 ounces. It was not until 1954 that meat rationing was finally abolished and consumption of carcase meat rose sharply reaching over 19 ounces in 1956. Since then there has been steady decline in the quantity of carcase meat purchased. In particular, the quantities purchased of beef and sheepmeat have declined while there has been a relatively small increase in pork consumption. These declines have to be viewed, however, against a switch to meat products and the fact that carcase meat is increasingly sold with less bone and more fat removed. In fact, purchases of meat in total still represent some 28 per cent of household food expenditure,

Figure 4.7
Consumption of meats

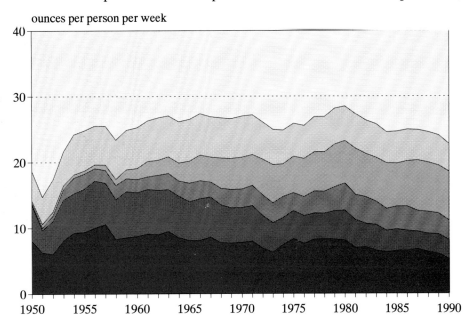

ounces per person per week

Bacon and ham
Poultry
Pork
Mutton and lamb
Beef and veal

about the same proportion as in the 1950s. The very rapid expansion of the poultry industry has contributed to this position with consumption of poultrymeat more than doubling in the last 25 years.

Fruit

Although fruit was not rationed during the war, supplies were very much reduced and per capita consumption of fresh fruit fell below 7 ounces per person per week. By the mid 1950s, consumption had risen to nearly 20 ounces and has continued to increase but at a very much slower rate. In addition, however, consumption of fruit juice has risen from negligible levels to over 7 fluid ounces per person per week. Throughout the period, apples, pears, bananas and oranges have remained the predominant fresh fruit consumed and still account for three quarters of purchases by weight (Figure 4.8). There is no doubt, however, that the range of fresh fruit available has expanded enormously. Varieties other than oranges now account for nearly 40 per cent of citrus purchases, peaches and nectarines have partially replaced plums and kiwi fruit are widely available alongside many types of exotic fruit. One product rapidly disappearing from the average diet is rhubarb whose consumption has fallen from 0.7 ounces per capita per week to less than 0.2 ounces.

Figure 4.8
Consumption of fruit

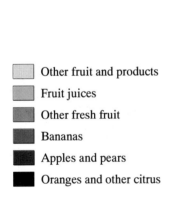

Other fruit and products
Fruit juices
Other fresh fruit
Bananas
Apples and pears
Oranges and other citrus

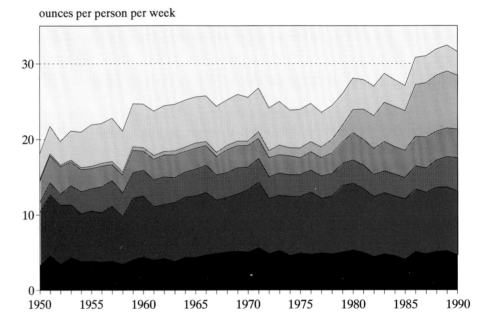

Vegetables

Among the vegetables, potatoes remain central to the British diet. When the survey started, consumption of potatoes was nearly 70 ounces per person per week, more than half of total vegetable consumption by weight; today the figure is just under a half. During the war, land was diverted to vegetable production and consumption of potatoes and field vegetables rose sharply (Figure 4.9). In the immediate postwar years, the increased availability of other foods led to a steady decline in purchases of potatoes. At the same time, there was some switching away from the traditional vegetables such as cabbage, brussels sprouts and root vegetables. In particular, during the 1960s, technology and the advent of the home freezer led to a surge in consumption of frozen vegetables. In recent years, the trend has been towards other fresh green and leafy salad vegetables and, as with fruit, the range of new and exotic varieties recorded in the Survey has increased enormously. Thus, while the total weight of vegetables, excluding potatoes, has increased only very slowly, the proportion of total household food expenditure has increased from some 7 per cent in the mid 1960s to nearly 12 per cent today.

Figure 4.9
Consumption of vegetables

Potatoes

Fresh green vegetables

Other fresh vegetables

Frozen vegetables and vegetable products

Other processed vegetables and vegetable products

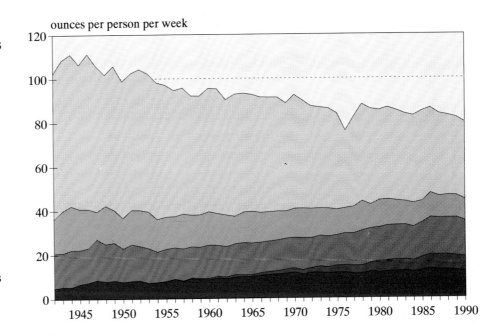

ounces per person per week

39

Regional comparisons

The second report of the National Food Survey Committee, *Studies in Urban Household Diets 1944-49*[1], sought to compare 1949 results from the survey for different regions of England and Wales, albeit for the urban working-class households to which the data related. Seven regions were identified, with London as a separate region. Since the sample was too small for separate analysis, households in Wales were split between the North West and South West regions.

Some interesting results arose from this early regional analysis. Londoners had a high consumption of milk and fruit but ate less bread and cakes than others. Southerners in general ate more vegetables, except potatoes, and the highest consumption of fresh vegetables was in the South and East. Egg consumption was also high in the South and East, but low prices there meant that expenditure per head was well below average. The South West and Midland regions shared high potato and low fish consumptions, although the Midland region was described as nearer to the national averages for the main food groups than any other. Northern regions tended to consume lower levels of milk, cheese, eggs, potatoes, other vegetables, fruit, sugar and preserves. Purchases of chips were much higher, however, and cooked fish consumption was twice as high in the North East than in any other region. Flour consumption was also high in the North East. In Scotland, prices tended to be higher and consumption levels were the lowest for rationed meat, eggs, fish, vegetables other than potatoes, fruit, fats and beverages. However, consumption of unrationed meat and bread was particularly high in Scotland.

In *Domestic Food Consumption and Expenditure: 1955*[2], geographical differences in the household diet were investigated more fully, and this analysis has been performed annually since then. The regional boundaries have changed over the years and the number of regions for analysis increased from 9 in 1955 to 10 in 1958 and 11 in 1960. There was further restructuring back to 9 regions in 1967 and this has formed the basis of geographical analyses since then. Figure 4.10 shows the regional structure in 1960 and in the present time. Prior to 1960 the Northern region was merged with East and West Ridings, and before 1958 the North Midlands and Eastern Regions were combined. London conurbation results are still available separately, but the data have been included in the South East/East Anglia region for the regional analyses.

1   Ministry of Agriculture, Fisheries and Food, *Studies in Urban Household Diets 1944-49 - Second Report of the National Food Survey Committee*, HMSO, 1956
2   Ministry of Agriculture, Fisheries and Food, *Domestic Food Consumption and Expenditure: 1955 - Annual Report of the National Food Survey Committee*, HMSO, 1957

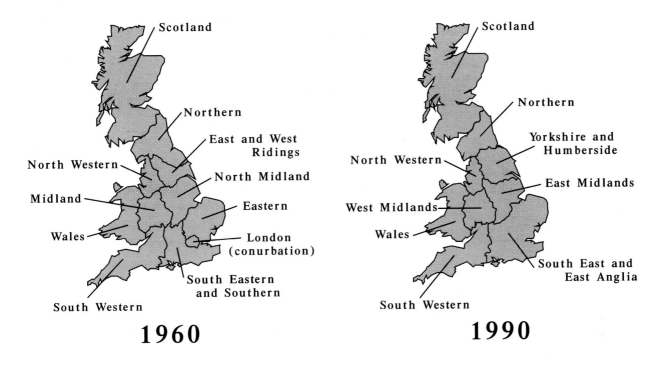

Figure 4.10
Regions for analysis

Figure 4.11
Vegetable consumption by region, 1960 and 1990

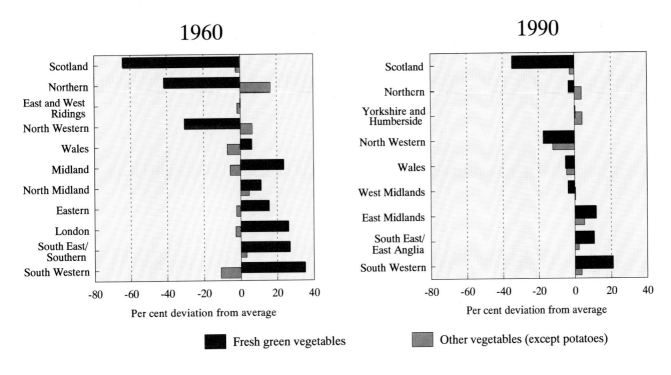

The National Food Survey continues to identify a number of strong regional differences in the diet of British households. However better communications, more uniform prices and changing tastes have all contributed to a degree of convergence in consumption levels. An example is given in Figure 4.11. Consumption of fresh green vegetables in 1960 was markedly higher in the southern regions than in the north, and especially Scotland. Consumption of other vegetables (excluding potatoes) and vegetable products was, if anything, the reverse. The regional pattern for green vegetables is still the same in 1990, but is far less marked. A strong regional pattern used to exist in the consumption of fats (Figure 4.12). Margarine consumption was high in the northern regions of Britain in 1960 and somewhat lower in Wales, London and the western regions. Butter consumption showed the opposite pattern. By 1990, some trends have been reversed. There is also the influence of low and reduced fat spreads, which are more popular in the south than the north.

Figure 4.12
Fat consumption by region, 1960 and 1990

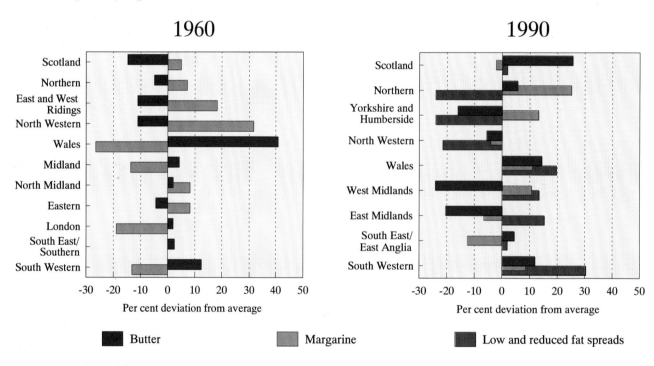

Income group comparisons

Since the Survey became nationally representative, it has been useful to analyse households by the income group of the head of household. It is not possible to make precise comparisons of income groups over time, because there have been changes in the definitions used. Not only have the target (and achieved) proportions of the sample in each income group varied, but the number and definitions of the groups have changed too. Thus in 1952 there were five groups, A, B, C, D (non-OAP) and D(OAP), to which all households were allocated. Non-earners were not distinguished from earners.

Table 4.13
Income groups in 1952

Income group	Income band	Percentage of survey households
	gross weekly income	%
A	£13 or more	8.4
B	£8 to £13	26.9
C	£4 10s to £8	40.0
D (non-OAP)	Under £4 10s	17.5
D (OAP)	" "	7.3

In 1953 the category D (non-OAP) was further subdivided into earners (now category D) and non-earners (now E2), and category A was subdivided in 1955. The higher-income non-earners, now E1, were included in categories A, B or C until 1974.

For comparison with the table above, in 1990 the classification was as follows:

Table 4.14
Income groups in 1990

Income group	Income band	Percentage of survey households
	gross weekly income	%
A1	£645 or more	3.1
A2	£475 to £645	5.0
B	£250 to £475	32.0
C	£125 to £250	25.1
D	Less than £125	5.0
E1	£125 or more	5.0
E2	Less than £125	13.7
OAP	na	11.1

Because of these classification changes, the charts which follow need to be interpreted with some care; they are included for illustrative purposes only.

Figure 4.15 compares expenditure on the major food groups in 1952 and 1990 by income group. Expenditure on meat and fish continues to account for the largest proportion of household food expenditure in all income groups, although expenditure on eggs has fallen in all cases. Expenditure on fruit and vegetables has risen proportionally more in higher-earning income groups than in lower income groups. Fruit is relatively cheap in 1990 so that the proportion of expenditure on fruit has fallen in some cases despite greatly increased consumption. Expenditure on cheese and miscellaneous items such as sauces and ice cream has risen in all income groups. The proportions spent on bread and cereal products, sugars and preserves and on fats have reduced for each income group. Expenditure on sugars and preserves and on cheese and eggs shows more variation with respect to income in 1990. The highest average expenditure for many food groups occurs in the higher-income non-earner group E1, which in 1990 comprised 5.0 per cent of households sampled. A possible explanation for this phenomenon is given on page 17.

Figure 4.15
Expenditure on main food groups by income group, 1952 and 1990

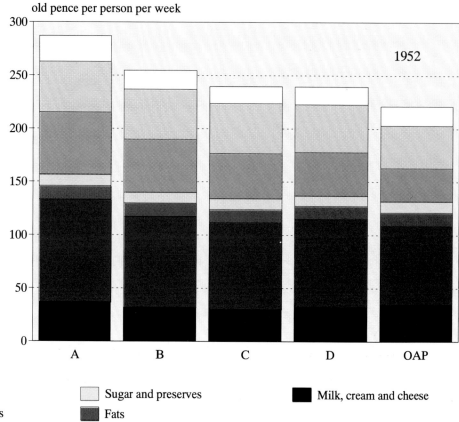

old pence per person per week

1952

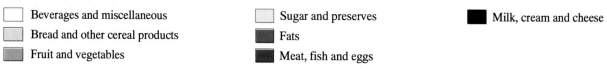

☐ Beverages and miscellaneous	☐ Sugar and preserves	■ Milk, cream and cheese
☐ Bread and other cereal products	▨ Fats	
▨ Fruit and vegetables	▨ Meat, fish and eggs	

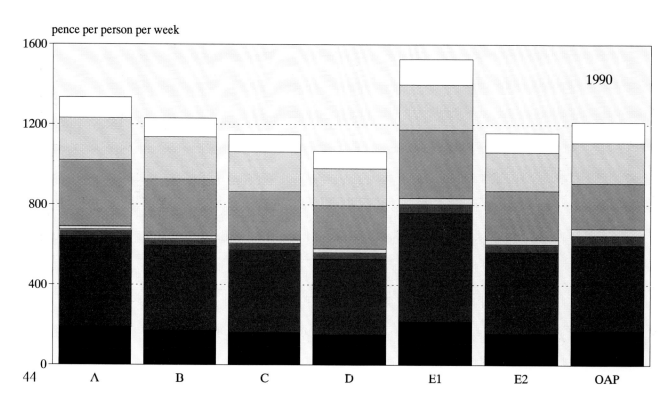

pence per person per week

1990

The following charts show the consumption of selected foods for each income group measured as the percentage deviation from the all-households average for each year. In Figure 4.16 it is particularly noticeable that households in income group A, which used to have above average consumption of milk and cream, now consume slightly below average, while for old-age pensioners and the unemployed, the trend is firmly in the other direction.

Figure 4.16
Consumption of milk and cream by income group

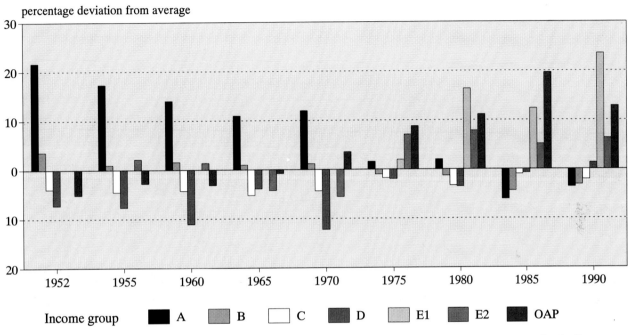

There is a similar pattern for eggs, but with more marked divergence since 1975 (Figure 4.17).

Figure 4.17
Consumption of eggs by income group

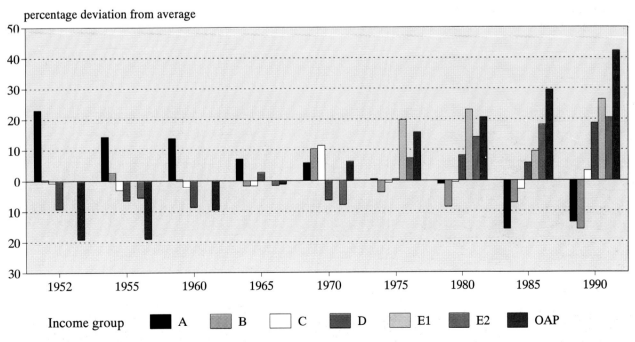

45

The rationing of sugar during the war resulted in very little difference in average levels of consumption of sugar and preserves between households from different income groups. Figure 4.18 shows subsequent steady divergence, with consumption in income groups A and B falling below the average, and for D, E1, E2 and pensioners rising higher above it. By 1990, pensioner households consumed 82 per cent more sugar and preserves than the average, and group A households consumed 30 per cent less.

Figure 4.18
Consumption of sugar and preserves by income group

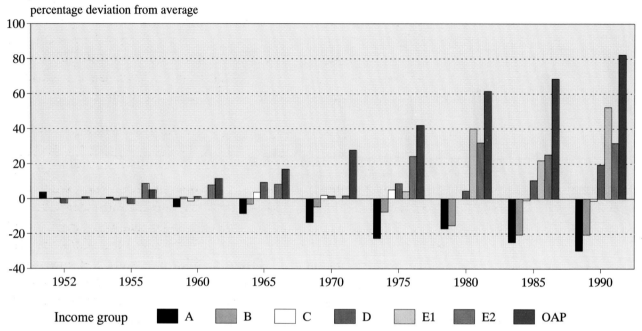

Fruit and fruit products, in contrast, show a reasonably consistent pattern over time, dominated by the high consumption level of the higher-income non-earners E1 since this category was introduced (Figure 4.19).

Figure 4.19
Consumption of fruit and fruit products by income group

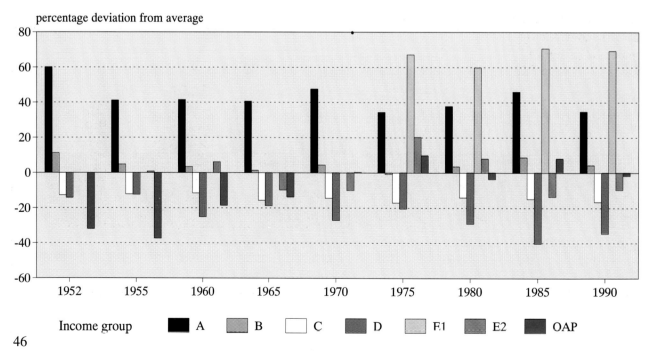

Household composition comparisons

There have been a number of changes in the composition of households in Britain over the last 50 years. The average number of persons in National Food Survey households rose slightly after the war, from 3.44 in 1942 to 3.62 in 1949, due largely to the increased number of children but tempered by the tendency for returning soldiers to set up new households. Since 1949 the average number of persons per household has steadily declined to just 2.62 in 1990. Within this total the proportion of children under 14 years has declined from 29 per cent in 1949 to 20 per cent in 1990. The Survey households also reflect an ageing of the population, with the proportions of men aged 65 and over and women aged 60 and over increasing from 4.2 per cent and 8.5 per cent respectively in 1953 to 5.7 per cent and 9.8 per cent in 1990. These, and other, demographic changes have had a significant effect on household food consumption and expenditure.

The classifications by household composition have also changed over the period of the Survey. Before 1972, adolescents aged 14 to 20 years until 1970 and 15 to 17 years thereafter, were categorised separately from younger children. Analyses of two-adult households with 0, 1, 2, 3 or 4 or more children have therefore excluded adolescent children until 1972 and, in addition, assume one male and one female adult before this date. In the category with no children, the adults are also expressly under the age of 55 prior to 1972. These factors may cause some discontinuities in the data presented. The following charts show the percentage deviation of the weekly expenditure per person in each type of household from the average for all households.

Households without children have been categorised by number of adults since 1972. As Figure 4.20 shows, the total household food expenditure of 1 and 2-adult households was around 20 per cent above the all-household average in each of the years shown, while large adult-only households spent only marginally above the average.

Figure 4.20
Expenditure per person on all household food by number of people in adult-only households

Number of adults

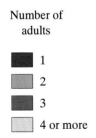

- 1
- 2
- 3
- 4 or more

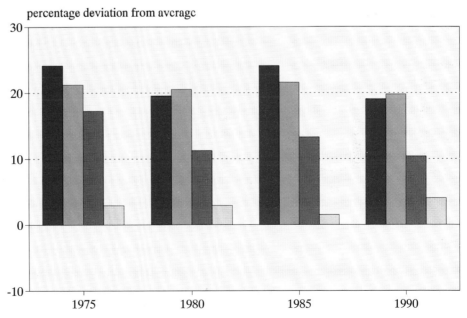

Expenditure on meat shows a different pattern, with 2 and 3-adult households spending well above average in 1975 (Figure 4.21). This difference has reduced over time, whereas the larger households now tend to spend more.

Figure 4.21
Expenditure per person on meat and meat products in adult-only households

Number of adults

1
2
3
4 or more

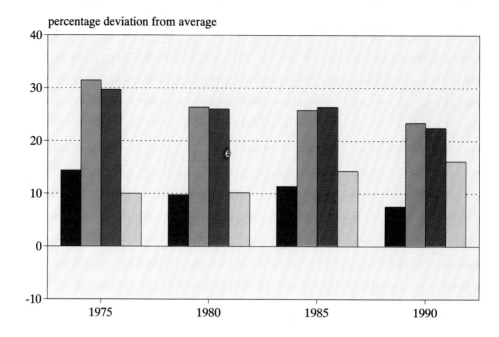

Expenditure on fish shows growing diversity, increasing with smaller households, and with fish apparently markedly less popular in larger families (Figure 4.22).

Figure 4.22
Expenditure per person on fish in adult-only households

Number of adults

1
2
3
4 or more

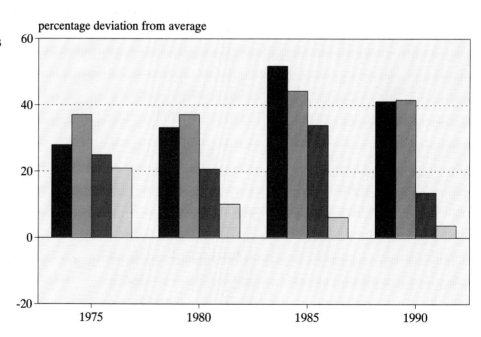

Figure 4.23 shows the pattern for household food expenditure in two-adult households with increasing numbers of children. Households with one child had near-average expenditure, while those with large numbers of

children spent considerably less. These patterns show considerable stability over time.

Figure 4.23
Expenditure per person on all food in 2-adult households with children.

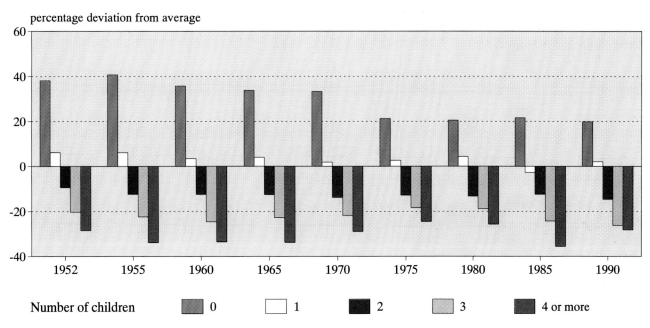

Expenditure per person on eggs shows considerable variation by number of children in the household especially following the removal of consumer subsidies in 1953. At that time large families spent significantly less per person on eggs than small families, but this pattern is now less marked although children clearly still eat fewer eggs from household supplies than adults.

Figure 4.24
Expenditure per person on eggs in 2-adult households with children

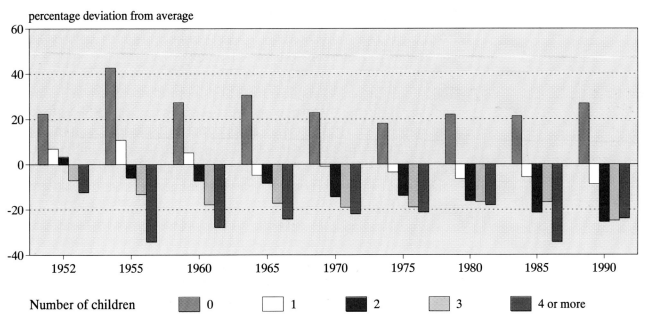

49

Fruit shows an even more pronounced expenditure pattern, with the highest expenditure in households with no children (55 per cent above average in 1952), and the lowest in those with the most children (43 per cent below average). There has been only a slight reduction in this large range over time.

Figure 4.25
Expenditure per person on fruit in 2-adult households with children

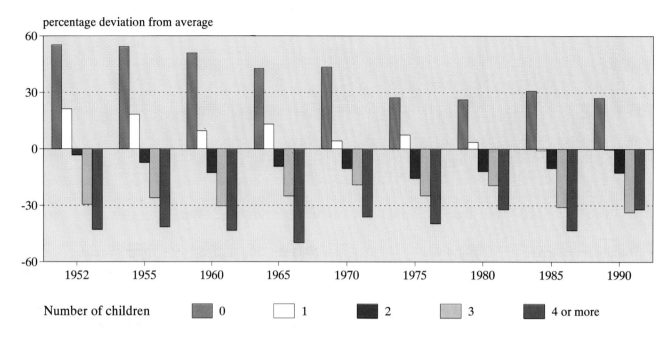

Seasonality

Many foods show seasonal consumption patterns, in part due to seasonality of supply and to the resulting price variations, but also due to seasonal changes in demand. Some of these seasonal patterns have changed considerably over time, others not at all.

Today only fresh vegetables, fresh fruit, and to some extent fresh fish and shellfish are regarded as truly seasonal. In 1950, quarterly consumption of eggs showed a very marked seasonal pattern with a range from 5 per person per week in the spring to only 2 in the autumn. This pattern changed as intensive egg production methods became widespread, and within a few years the range of variation was greatly reduced (Figure 4.26).

Figure 4.26
Seasonal variation in consumption of eggs

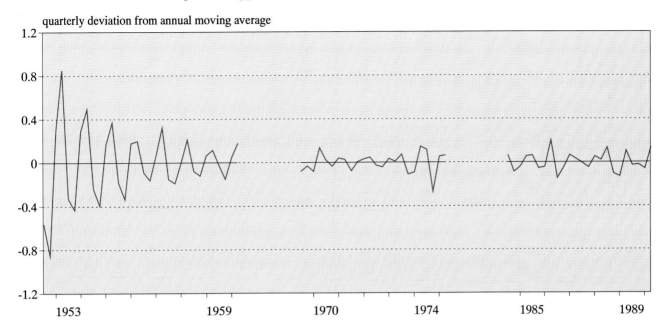

Many fresh vegetables retain a considerable seasonal element (Figure 4.27). Potatoes, for example, show no reduction in seasonal variation despite declining consumption overall. However, fresh peas and beans, which accounted for half of all fresh green vegetable consumption by weight during July and August 1950, now only make a small contribution.

Figure 4.27
Seasonal variation in consumption of fresh green vegetables

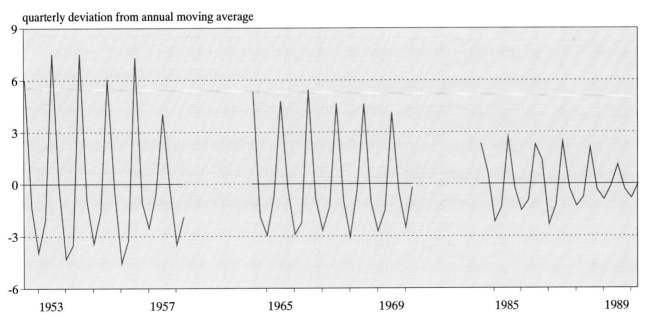

Fresh fruit consumption, although still highly seasonal in many respects, has been influenced by improved storage and by increased sources of supply. Figure 4.28 shows how the consumption pattern for apples has become much less pronounced over time.

Figure 4.28
Seasonal variation in consumption of apples

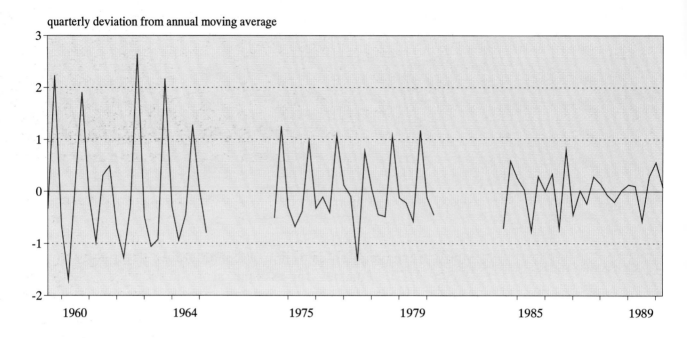

Convenience foods

One particularly notable feature of the last few decades has been the marked increase in the variety of convenience foods available. The Survey classifies these into three main groups: canned and bottled (or similarly packaged), frozen, and 'other', including for example breakfast cereals, biscuits and custard powder.

Consumption of vegetable and fruit juices has risen strongly since 1972, particularly in the period 1976 - 1988 (Figure 4.29). Other canned and bottled convenience foods show less marked changes, with a small increase for fish and slight declines for fruit, cereal products and 'other' foods.

52

Figure 4.29
Consumption of canned and
bottled convenience foods

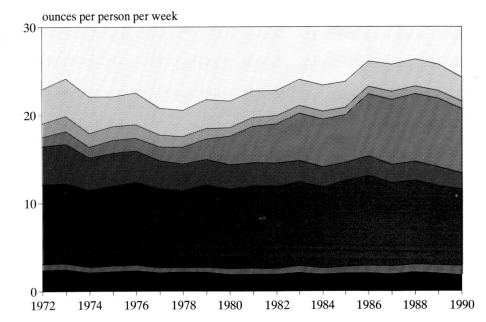

ounces per person per week

Other convenience foods

Cereal products

Vegetable and fruit juices

Fruit

Vegetables

Fish and fish products

Meat and meat products

Most frozen foods, however, show very marked upward trends over this period. Consumption of frozen cereal products (such as pizzas, gateaux and cheesecakes) have risen eightfold, from 0.15 ounces per person per week in 1972 to 1.21 ounces in 1990. Frozen meat products and vegetables also show strong increases (Figure 4.30), and frozen vegetables account for 60 per cent by weight of all frozen convenience foods.

Figure 4.30
Consumption of frozen
convenience foods

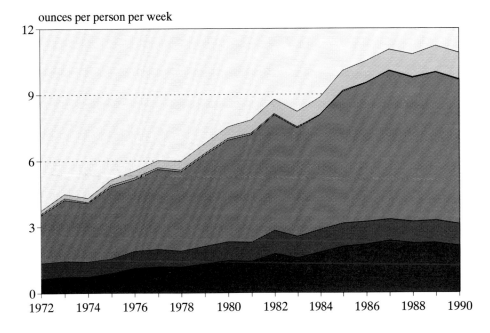

ounces per person per week

Cereal products

Fruit and fruit products

Vegetables

Fish and fish products

Meat and meat products

Other convenience foods show little change, with only slight increases for meat and meat products, vegetables and other foods. Although consumption of cereal convenience foods was no higher in 1990 than in the early 1970s, consumption of breakfast cereals has risen from 20 per cent of this group in 1972 to 30 per cent in 1990.

Figure 4.31
Consumption of other convenience foods

Other convenience foods

Cereal products

Vegetables

Fish and fish products

Meat and meat products

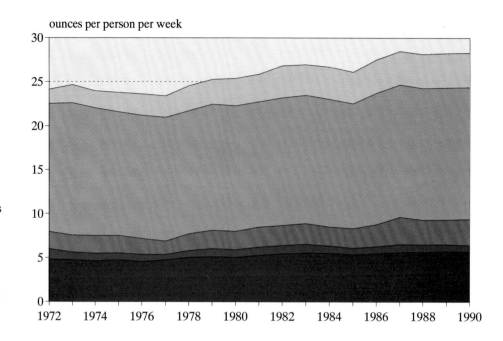

Free food

The value per person per week of food obtained free has declined from 3.8 per cent of the total value of all food in 1952 to 1.9 per cent in 1990. The most marked decline is for eggs (Figure 4.32). The peaks for potatoes in 1958 and 1976 are due to the effect on prices of poor crops in those years, and free supplies of fresh green vegetables and other vegetables also peaked in 1975 - 1977.

Figure 4.32
Value of 'free' food as a percentage of total value of all food

Fresh fruit

Other vegetables

Fresh green vegetables

Potatoes

Eggs

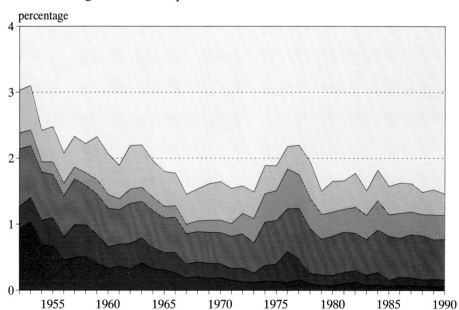

Nutrient intakes

Trends in the average nutrient intake recorded in the Survey between 1940 and 1990 are shown in Appendix C Table 8. Although the survey has been conducted in a consistent way throughout the 50 years, the trends should still be interpreted with some caution. The first reason for this is that although the survey sample has been representative of the whole of Great Britain since 1950, the sample between 1940 and 1949 was drawn only from urban working class households. The second arises because the nutrient composition of many foods had changed with time, largely as a result of changes in agricultural or food manufacturing practice. Many of these changes are incorporated as they occur, but some can only be included after they have been properly quantified in major analytical studies. The largest break in series occurred in 1974, when the amounts of fat, iron and several other nutrients in carcase meat (which is an important source of nutrients) were thoroughly revised to reflect changes that had begun many years earlier. A further factor to be borne in mind is that all these values refer to the nutritional value of the diet as bought, although there is a standard adjustment for waste. There will have been changes in domestic cooking practice which could have affected the amounts of nutrients actually eaten.

Figure 4.33
Nutritional value of household food supplies

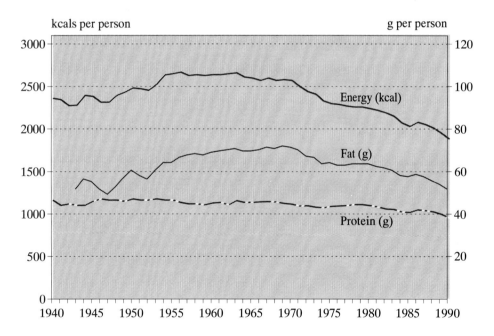

Trends in the total amount of food, apart from sweets and alcohol, used by households throughout Britain are best seen from the trends in energy (calorie) value. This was at its lowest in 1942 and 1943, but then rose steadily from 2,270 kcal per person per day to more than 2,600 kcal between 1954 and 1964 (Figure 4.33). It then declined steadily until it is now less than 1900 kcal per person per day, reflecting both a lower energy need in an increasingly sedentary population and a reduction in the contribution which eating at home makes to people's total energy needs.

This energy comes from the fat, protein and carbohydrate in the foods, and the changing proportion which each has contributed since the early 1940s is shown in Figure 4.34. After the Second World War, and particularly as a free choice of food became available again after the end of food rationing, the contribution made by carbohydrate dropped and that from fat rose even though the absolute level of fat has fallen markedly. The proportion of energy from fat has been at its current level of about 42 per cent for 20 years, and has not been as low as the recommended level of 35 per cent since 1948. Until recently, much of the fat in the household diet was saturated because it came mainly from beef, lamb, dairy fats and heavily hydrogenated margarines. The fatty acid composition of the diet was not determined until the early 1970s, but the amount of saturated fatty acids has declined steadily since then, while the amount of polyunsaturated fatty acids has risen.

Figure 4.34
Percentage of energy
from carbohydrate,
fat and protein

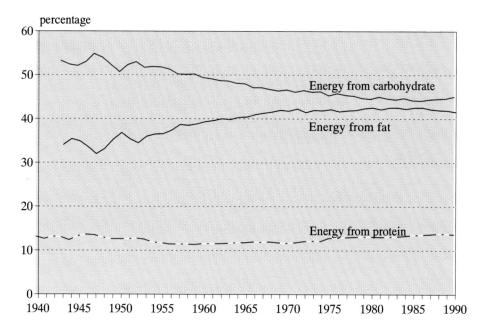

There have also been changes in the amounts of vitamins and minerals. Calcium intakes rose in 1943 when flour was first required by law to be fortified with this nutrient as well as with iron, thiamin and niacin. The importance of (white) bread and milk in the British diet meant that calcium intakes stayed high for many years, but because the importance of both has declined the calcium content of the diet dropped from more then 1000 milligrams (mg) per day throughout the 1950s and 1960s to only 820 mg per person per day in 1990. The intake of most other nutrients recorded in the Survey also has fallen with the gradual decline in the amount of food eaten in the home, but that of vitamin C has remained steady. This is largely because of the rapid increase in the contribution made by fruit juices, which has offset the decline from the traditional main source, which is potatoes.

More details of the main sources of each nutrient over time, and of the nutritional value of the diet in households in different regions and income groups and with different family composition, can be found in previous Annual Reports.

Structure of the Survey

Introduction

The National Food Survey is a continuous sampling enquiry into the domestic food consumption and expenditure of private households in Great Britain. Each household which participates does so voluntarily, and without payment, for one week only. By regularly changing the households surveyed, information is obtained continuously throughout the year apart from a short break at Christmas.

Information provided by households

The sole informant in each household is the person, female or male, principally responsible for domestic arrangements. For convenience, that person is referred to as the main 'diary-keeper'. She (or he) keeps a record, with guidance from an interviewer, of all the food intended for human consumption entering the home each day; the Survey therefore excludes meals out and pet food. The following details are noted for each food item: the description, the quantity (in either imperial or metric units) and - in respect of purchases - the cost. Food obtained free from a farm or other business owned by a household member or from a garden or allotment is recorded only at the time it is used. To avoid the double counting of purchases, gifts of food are excluded if they were bought by the donating households. Also excluded from the Survey are a few items which individual family members often buy for themselves without coming to the attention of the diary-keeper - the Survey's sole informant; these are chocolates, sugar confectionery, and soft and alcoholic drinks[1].

As well as the detail about the foods entering the household, the diary-keeper also notes which persons (including visitors) are present at each meal together with a description of the type (but not the quantities) of food served. This enables an approximate check to be made between the foods served and those acquired during the week. Records are also kept of the number and nature (whether lunch, dinner, etc) of the meals obtained outside the home by each member of the household; this is used in the nutritional calculations - see below. No information is currently collected, however, about the cost or composition of meals taken outside the home although, exceptionally, the quantity of school milk consumed by children is recorded.

---

1 Since 1975, particulars have been obtained of soft drinks bought for the household supply. The results are presented in the Annual Report but the information is excluded from the main analyses because of the likelihood of bias from under-recording.

Finally, on a separate questionnaire, details are entered of the characteristics of the family and its members but names are not collected. The identities of addresses are strictly confidential. They are known only to those who were involved respectively with selecting the sample and carrying out the fieldwork. They are not even divulged to the Ministry of Agriculture, Fisheries and Food which is responsible for analysing and reporting the Survey results.

As the Survey records only the quantities of food entering the household and not the amount actually consumed, it cannot provide meaningful frequency distributions of households classified according to levels of food eaten or of nutrition. However, averaged over sufficient households, the quantities recorded should equate with consumption (in the widest possible sense, including waste food discarded or fed to pets) provided purchasing habits are not upset and there is no general accumulation or depletion of household food stocks.

The National Food Survey is selected to be representative of mainland Great Britain (including the Isle of Wight but not the Scilly Isles nor the islands of Scotland). In 1990 a three-stage stratified random sampling scheme was used, the first stage of which involved the selection of local authority districts as the primary sampling units (P.S.U's). As in previous years, an eighth of the local authority districts were retired and replaced each quarter (re-selection being possible) and once selected, remained in the Survey for eight consecutive quarters before being retired. The number of local authority districts included in the Survey for sampling purposes was 52 at any one time.

The second stage of the selection procedure in 1990 involved the selection of postal sectors within each of the districts. In 1990 the sample size was reduced by approximately 6 per cent compared with 1989. This was achieved by reducing the number of postal sectors sampled in each Local Authority District from 16 to 15. The third stage the selection of 18 delivery points from each postal sector. The delivery points were drawn from the Small Users Postcode Address File (PAF) using interval sampling from a random origin.

The 52 local authority districts selected are randomly divided into two sets of 26. The two sets are worked in alternate 21 day intervals with two postal sectors covered during each 21 day interval. Thus, in the first interval, 52 postal sectors from one set of 26 local authority districts are worked and in the second 21 day interval 52 postal sectors from the other set are worked.

The local authority districts surveyed in 1990 are listed in Table 1 of this Appendix. At the second stage of sampling 786 postal sectors were selected and at the third stage 14,148 addresses. When visited, a few of these addresses were found to be those of institutions or other establishments not eligible for inclusion in the Survey; others were unoccupied or had been demolished. In addition, some addresses were found to contain more than one household. After allowing for these factors, the estimated eligible number of households in the sample was 12,238. In some households the diary-keeper was seen but refused to give any information, a number of other diary-keepers answered a questionnaire[2] but declined to keep a week's record, while some who undertook to keep a record did not in fact complete it. Finally, a few records were lost in the post or were rejected at the editing stage leaving a responding sample of 7,205 households representing 59 per cent of the eligible sample. Details are as follows:-

	Households	Households selected (%)
Number of households at the address selected in the sample	12,238	100
Number that could not be visited for operational reasons	1	...
Number visited but no contact made with the diary-keeper	1,547	13
(Number of households where diary-keeper contacted)	(10,690)	(87)
Diary-keeper seen but refused to give any information	1,787	15
Diary-keeper answered a questionnaire but declined to keep a week's record	771	6
Diary-keeper started to keep a week's record but did not complete it	846	7
Completed records lost in the post or rejected at the editing stage	81	1
Number of responding households	7,205	59

Nutritional analysis of survey results

The energy value and nutrient content of food obtained for consumption in the home[3] are evaluated using special tables for food composition. The nutrient conversion factors were originally based on values given in *The Composition of Foods*[4] but are thoroughly revised each year for two reasons. First, to reflect changes in nutrient values resulting from new methods of food production, handling and fortification. Second, to reflect changes in the structure of the food categories used in the Survey - for example changes in the relative importance of the many products grouped under 'breakfast cereals'.

2   The questionnaire relates to family composition, occupation, etc.

3   See the 2nd paragraph of this Appendix and 'Food obtained for consumption' in the Glossary.

4   A A Paul and D A T Southgate. *McCance and Widdowson's The Composition of Foods*, 4th edition, Ministry of Agriculture, Fisheries and Food and Medical Research Council, HMSO, 1978

The nutrient factors used make allowance for inedible materials such as the bones in meat and the outer leaves and skins of vegetables. For certain foods, such as potatoes and carrots, allowance is also made for seasonal variations in this wastage and/or nutrient content. Further allowance is made for the expected cooking losses of thiamin and vitamin C; average thiamin retention factors are applied to appropriate items within each major food group and the (weighted) average loss over the *whole* diet is estimated to be about 20 per cent. The losses of vitamin C are set at 75 per cent for green vegetables and 50 per cent for other vegetables. However, no allowance is made for wastage of *edible* food. The exception is when the adequacy of the diet is being assessed in comparison with recommended intakes (see the final paragraph of this Appendix). Then, the assumption is made that in each type of household, 10 per cent of all foods - and hence of all nutrients available for consumption - is either lost through wastage or spoilage in the kitchen or on the plate, or fed to domestic pets[5].

The energy content of the food is calculated from the protein, fat and available carbohydrate (expressed as monosaccharide) contents using the respective conversion factors, 4, 9 and 3.75 kcal per gram. It is expressed both in kilocalories and megajoules (1,000 kcal = 4.184 MJ). Niacin is expressed both as free niacin and as niacin equivalent; the latter value includes one-sixtieth of the tryptophan content of the protein in the food. Vitamin A activity is expressed as micrograms of retinol equivalent, that is the sum of the weights of retinol and one-sixth of the β-carotene. Fatty acids are grouped according to the number of double bonds present, that is into saturated, monounsaturated and polyunsaturated fatty acids. For the diet as a whole, the total fatty acids constitute about 95 per cent of the weight of the fat. This proportion varies slightly for individual foods, being lower for dairy fats with their greater content of short-chain acids and a little higher for most other foods.

The nutritional results are tabulated in two main ways for each category of household in the Survey —

(a) *Per person*. This presentation is directly comparable to the per person presentation in Section 2 of this Report of the amounts of food obtained. However, it has some drawbacks where the interpretation of nutrient intakes is concerned. It does not take into account contributions made by meals outside the home or by food outside the diary-keepers' purview (see the 2nd paragraph of this Appendix). Nor is any allowance made for the wastage of edible food. The averages

---

5 An enquiry into the amounts of potentially edible food which are thrown away or fed to pets in Great Britain recorded an average wastage of about 6 per cent of households' food supplies (see R W Wenlock, D H Buss, B J Derry and E J Dixon, *British Journal of Nutrition, 43*, 1980, pp 53-70). However, this is considered likely to be a minimum estimate, and the conventional Survey deduction of 10 per cent has been retained thereby preserving continuity with previous years.

per person can also be misleading. For example, average per caput energy intakes in families with small children are invariably less than those for wholly adult households; but this does not by itself indicate that the former are less well nourished because children have a smaller absolute need for energy.

(b) *As a proportion of intakes recommended by DHSS* [6] Some of the above drawbacks are overcome in this presentation. It involves comparing intakes with household needs after the age, sex and occupational activity of each member have been taken into account. Allowance is also made for meals eaten outside the home and for the presence of visitors by redefining, in effect, the number of people consuming the household food - *not* by adding or subtracting estimates of the nutrient content of the meals in question. Moreover, for these comparisons, the estimated energy and nutrient contents are reduced throughout by 10 per cent to allow for wastage of edible food (see footnote on the previous page).

---

6 Department of Health and Social Security, *Recommended Daily Amounts of Food Energy and Nutrients for Groups of People in the United Kingdom*-Reports on Health and Social Subjects No. 15, HMSO, 1979. These recommendations have been adapted slightly for use in the National Food Survey.

Table 1
Local Authority Districts
surveyed in 1990

Region[a]	Definition of region[a]	Local Authority Districts[b] selected in the sample for 1990
England: North	Cleveland, Cumbria, Durham, Northumberland, Tyne and Wear	Langbaurgh *Sunderland Tynedale
Yorkshire and Humberside	Humberside, North Yorkshire, South Yorkshire, West Yorkshire	*Leeds *Rotherham *Sheffield *Bradford East Yorkshire *Wakefield
North West	Cheshire, Lancashire, Greater Manchester, Merseyside	*Stockport *Knowsley Chester *Liverpool *Bury Hyndburn Ribble Valley *Tameside
East Midllands	Derbyshire, Leicestershire, Lincolnshire, Northamptonshire, Nottinghamshire	Derby Harborough Charnwood
West Midlands	Hereford and Worcester, Shropshire, Staffordshire, Warwickshire, West Midlands	*Sandwell Bromsgrove *Birmingham Tamworth Bridgenorth Cannock Chase Stafford Stoke-on-Trent
South West	Avon, Cornwall, Devon, Dorset, Gloucestershire, Somerset, Wiltshire	Bristol Yeovil Poole Mid Devon Torridge
East Anglia	Cambridgeshire, Norfolk, Suffolk	Broadland East Cambridgeshire
South East	Greater London, Bedfordshire, Berkshire, Buckhinghamshire, East Sussex, Essex, Hampshire, Hertfordshire, Isle of Wight, Kent, Oxfordshire, West Sussex	*Lambeth *Newham *Croydon *Hillingdon *Southwark *Merton *Barnet *Camden *Lewisham *Hounslow Hove Broxbourne Dacorum Tandridge Wealden Oxford

Table 1 *continued*

Region[a]	Definition of region[a]	Local Authority Districts[b] selected in thesample for 1990
South East (continued)		Thurrock Colchester South Oxfordshire Southend Lewes Winchester
Wales	The whole of Wales	Wrexham Maelor Islwyn Meirionnydd
Scotland	The whole of Scotland	*Glasgow Falkirk Wigtown *Hamilton Kyle and Carrick Banff and Buchan Edinburgh Badenock and Strathspey

(a) These are the standard regions as revised with effect from 1st April 1974.

(b) Local Authority Districts marked * are wholly or partly within Greater London, the Metropolitan districts, or the Central Clydeside conurbation.

Table 2

Distribution of the 1990 Survey sample according to income

Income group	Gross weekly income of head of household [a]	Number of households	Percentage of households in whole sample	in groups A1 to D realised	in groups A1 to D target
Households containing one or more earners [b]					
A1	£645 or more	222	3.1	4.4	3
A2	£475 and under £645	357	5.0	7.1	7
B	£250 and under £475	2,307	32.0	45.6	40
C	£125 and under £250	1,805	25.1	35.7	40
D	Less than £125	363	5.0	7.2	10
Total A1 to D		5,054	70.2	100	100
Households wiithout an earner [b]					
E1	£125 or more	360	5.0		
E2	Less than £125	991	13.7		
Pensioner households [c]					
OAP	na	800	11.1		
Total all households		7,205	100		

(a) Or of the principal earner if the income of the head of household was below £125 (the upper limit for group D).

(b) By convention, the short-term unemployed are classified as 'earners' until they have been out of work for more than a year when unemployment benefit ceases.

Table 3

Composition of the
sample of responding
households, 1990

	Households		Persons		Average number of persons per household	% of households owning a:	
	Number	%	Number	%		deep-freezer	micro-wave
All households	7,205	100	18,867	100	2.62	83	53
Analysis by region							
Scotland	598	8.3	1,597	8.5	2.67	81	51
Wales	433	6.0	1,132	6.0	2.61	80	55
England	6,174	85.7	16,138	85.5	2.61	83	53
North	424	5.9	1,126	6.0	2.66	78	54
Yorkshire and Humberside	679	9.4	1,733	9.2	2.55	77	54
North West	908	12.6	2,394	12.7	2.64	82	50
East Midlands	441	6.1	1,166	6.2	2.64	87	55
West Midlands	661	9.2	1,809	9.6	2.74	83	54
South West	627	8.7	1,616	8.6	2.58	83	54
South East/East Anglia	2,434	33.8	6,294	33.4	2.59	85	52
Analysis by income group (a)							
A1	222	3.1	714	3.8	3.22	93	68
A2	357	5.0	1,150	6.1	3.22	95	73
B	2,307	32.0	7,117	37.7	3.08	91	67
C	1,805	25.1	5,210	27.6	2.89	86	59
D	363	5.0	997	5.3	2.75	74	47
E1	360	5.0	634	3.4	1.76	83	38
E2	991	13.8	1,926	10.2	1.94	73	32
OAP	800	11.1	1,119	5.9	1.40	58	20

Analysis by household composition (b)

Number of adults	Number of children	Number	%	Number	%		deep-freezer	micro-wave
1	0	1,522	21.1	1,522	8.0	1.00	59	29
1	1 or more	261	3.6	720	3.8	2.76	78	42
2	0	2,383	33.1	4,766	25.3	2.00	85	53
2	1	629	8.7	1,887	10.0	3.00	91	67
2	2	878	12.2	3,512	18.6	4.00	94	67
2	3	297	4.1	1,485	7.9	5.00	96	67
2	4 or more	82	1.1	514	2.7	6.27	90	62
3	0	528	7.3	1,584	8.4	3.00	92	63
3 or more	1 or 2	361	5.0	1,653	8.8	4.58	97	68
3 or more	3 or more	45	0.6	307	1.6	6.82	91	67
4 or more	0	219	3.0	917	4.9	4.19	94	66

(a) For definition of income groups see Table 2 of this Appendix and the Glossary.

(b) See 'Adult' and 'Child' in the Glossary.

Appendix B

Supplementary Tables

List of supplementary tables

page

1. Household consumption of individual foods: quarterly and annual national averages, 1990   66

2. Household food prices for individual foods, 1988-1990   72

3. Soft drinks: purchases and expenditure, 1990   75

4. Meals eaten outside the home, 1990   76

5. Average number of mid-day meals per week per child aged 5-14 years, 1990   77

6. Household food consumption by main food groups, according to income group, 1990   78

7. Household food expenditure by main food groups, according to income group, 1990   80

8. Household food expenditure by main food groups, according to household composition, 1990   82

9. Household food consumption according to household composition groups within income groups: selected food items, 1990   84

10. Nutritional value of household food: national averages, 1988-1990   86

11. Nutritional value of household food in different regions, 1990   87

12. Nutritional value of household food in different income groups, 1990   88

13. Nutritional value of food in households of different composition, 1990   89

14. Contributions made by selected foods to the nutritional value of household food: national averages, 1990   90

Table 1

Household consumption of individual foods: quarterly and annual national averages, 1990

ounces per person per week, except where otherwise stated

			Consumption				Purchases	Percentage of all households purchasing each type of food during Survey week
		Jan/ March	April/ June	July/ Sept	Oct/ Dec	Yearly average	Yearly average	
MILK AND CREAM :								
Liquid wholemilk, full price[a]	(pt)	2.26	2.13	2.05	2.04	2.12	2.07	67
Welfare milk	(pt)	0.03	0.04	0.03	0.03	0.03	...	–
School milk	(pt)	0.01	0.01	0.01	0.02	0.01	0.01	1
Other milk	(pt)	0.03	0.05	0.04	0.04	0.04	0.04	9
Condensed milk	(eq pt)	0.05	0.05	0.04	0.05	0.05	0.05	6
Dried milk, branded	(eq pt)	0.06	0.07	0.06	0.05	0.06	0.06	1
Instant milk	(eq pt)	0.05	0.06	0.06	0.06	0.06	0.06	2
Yoghurt	(pt)	0.15	0.19	0.17	0.16	0.17	0.17	32
Skimmed milks[a]	(pt)	1.20	1.25	1.18	1.36	1.25	1.25	44
Cream	(pt)	0.02	0.03	0.03	0.02	0.02	0.02	13
Total milk and cream	(pt or eq pt)	**3.86**	**3.88**	**3.69**	**3.83**	**3.82**	**3.71**	**96**
CHEESE :								
Natural[a]		3.55	3.78	3.71	3.75	3.70	3.69	59
Processed		0.32	0.30	0.32	0.26	0.30	0.30	12
Total cheese		**3.87**	**4.08**	**4.04**	**4.01**	**4.00**	**4.00**	**62**
MEAT AND MEAT PRODUCTS :								
Carcase meat								
Beef and veal[a]		6.06	5.13	4.40	5.37	5.24	5.21	43
Mutton and lamb[a]		2.72	2.75	3.16	3.04	2.92	2.90	21
Pork[a]		3.21	3.30	2.56	2.80	2.97	2.95	27
Total carcase meat		**11.99**	**11.18**	**10.11**	**11.21**	**11.12**	**11.06**	**61**
Other meat and meat products								
Liver[a]		0.52	0.37	0.29	0.36	0.38	0.38	8
Offals, other than liver		0.18	0.11	0.07	0.11	0.12	0.12	2
Bacon and ham, uncooked[a]		3.10	3.03	2.84	3.12	3.02	3.02	46
Bacon and ham, cooked, including canned		1.02	1.26	1.21	1.09	1.15	1.14	36
Cooked poultry, not purchased in cans		0.38	0.54	0.65	0.52	0.52	0.52	11
Corned meat		0.62	0.66	0.67	0.61	0.64	0.64	17
Other cooked meat, not purchased in cans		0.36	0.42	0.41	0.34	0.38	0.38	15
Other canned meat and canned meat products		0.95	1.17	1.35	1.18	1.17	1.16	16
Broiler chicken, uncooked, including frozen		4.92	5.51	5.28	4.81	5.13	5.12	31
Other poultry, uncooked, including frozen[a]		1.95	2.83	1.85	2.58	2.30	2.30	10
Rabbit and other meat		0.05	0.02	0.04	0.03	0.04	0.03	...
Sausages, uncooked, pork		1.05	1.25	1.26	1.02	1.14	1.14	17
Sausages, uncooked, beef		1.44	1.39	0.98	1.26	1.27	1.26	17
Meat pies and sausage rolls, ready-to-eat[a]		0.52	0.65	0.53	0.57	0.57	0.57	14
Frozen convenience meats or frozen convenience meat products[a]		2.00	2.21	2.06	2.23	2.13	2.13	23
Other meat products[a]		2.95	3.18	3.02	3.02	3.04	3.04	43
Total other meat and meat products		**22.00**	**24.59**	**22.51**	**22.86**	**22.99**	**22.95**	**88**
Total meat and meat products		**33.99**	**35.77**	**32.62**	**34.07**	**34.11**	**34.01**	**91**
FISH :								
White, filleted, fresh		0.82	0.72	0.64	0.69	0.72	0.71	11
White, unfilleted, fresh		0.16	0.18	0.09	0.15	0.15	0.14	1
White, uncooked, frozen		0.65	0.77	0.70	0.55	0.67	0.67	9
Herrings, filleted, fresh		0.01	...	0.01	0.03	0.01	0.01	...
Herrings, unfilleted, fresh		0.03	0.02	0.02	0.02	0.02	0.02	...
Fat, fresh, other than herrings		0.18	0.29	0.27	0.23	0.24	0.24	3
White, processed		0.16	0.19	0.13	0.14	0.15	0.15	3
Fat, processed, filleted		0.15	0.21	0.14	0.16	0.17	0.17	4
Fat, processed, unfilleted		0.03	0.01	0.01	...	0.01	0.01	...
Shellfish		0.23	0.15	0.15	0.19	0.18	0.18	4
Cooked fish		0.53	0.48	0.63	0.53	0.54	0.54	13
Canned salmon		0.14	0.22	0.23	0.23	0.21	0.21	6
Other canned or bottled fish		0.67	0.95	0.88	0.75	0.82	0.82	20
Fish products, not frozen		0.21	0.25	0.22	0.20	0.22	0.22	8
Frozen convenience fish products		0.96	1.04	0.92	0.99	0.98	0.98	16
Total fish		**4.93**	**5.49**	**5.05**	**4.86**	**5.08**	**5.06**	**61**

Table 1 *continued*

ounces per person per week, except where otherwise stated

		Consumption					Purchases	Percentage of all households purchasing each type of food during Survey week
		Jan/ March	April/ Jun	July/ Sept	Oct/ Dec	Yearly average	Yearly average	
EGGS	(no)	2.18	2.35	2.13	2.15	2.20	2.12	51
FATS :								
Butter[a]		1.61	1.60	1.46	1.77	1.61	1.60	25
Margarine[a]		3.24	3.23	3.03	3.27	3.19	3.19	33
Lard and compound cooking fat		0.85	0.81	0.75	0.81	0.80	0.80	12
Vegetable and salad oils	(fl oz)	1.66	1.48	1.29	1.71	1.53	1.53	9
All other fats[a]		1.87	1.89	1.78	1.91	1.86	1.86	26
Total fats		9.23	9.01	8.31	9.46	9.00	9.00	69
SUGAR AND PRESERVES :								
Sugar		6.02	5.82	5.98	6.32	6.04	6.04	34
Jams, jellies and fruit curds		0.83	0.84	0.77	0.77	0.80	0.77	12
Marmalade		0.57	0.56	0.45	0.56	0.53	0.53	8
Syrup, treacle		0.17	0.16	0.15	0.16	0.16	0.16	2
Honey		0.22	0.20	0.17	0.21	0.20	0.19	3
Total sugar and preserves		7.80	7.57	7.53	8.01	7.73	7.69	46
VEGETABLES :								
Old potatoes								
January-August								
not prepacked		27.10	20.13	0.11	–	11.83	11.41	na
prepacked		8.42	5.54	0.09	–	3.51	3.51	na
New potatoes								
January-August								
not prepacked		0.07	7.50	17.51	–	6.27	5.76	na
prepacked		0.03	1.25	3.99	–	1.32	1.32	na
Potatoes								
September -December								
not prepacked		–	–	8.76	29.47	9.56	8.85	na
prepacked		–	–	2.32	8.40	2.68	2.68	na
Total fresh potatoes		35.62	34.42	32.78	37.87	35.17	33.53	
Cabbages, fresh		2.89	3.25	2.75	2.93	2.95	2.57	23
Brussels sprouts, fresh		1.94	0.07	0.14	1.83	0.99	0.89	10
Cauliflowers, fresh		1.80	2.65	1.92	2.70	2.27	2.17	19
Leafy salads, fresh		1.19	2.30	2.46	1.12	1.77	1.65	36
Peas, fresh		0.37	0.39	0.49	0.35	0.40	0.09	1
Beans, fresh		0.31	0.53	1.80	0.86	0.87	0.25	3
Other fresh green vegetables		0.49	0.58	0.49	0.56	0.53	0.44	8
Total fresh green vegetables		9.00	9.78	10.04	10.36	9.79	8.07	60
Carrots, fresh		4.37	3.52	3.26	4.54	3.92	3.61	38
Turnips and swedes, fresh		1.29	0.65	0.49	1.32	0.94	0.89	10
Other root vegetables, fresh		0.95	0.50	0.49	1.05	0.75	0.63	10
Onions, shallots, leeks, fresh		3.57	2.92	2.85	3.46	3.20	2.88	35
Cucumbers, fresh		0.81	1.57	1.56	0.78	1.18	1.13	25
Mushrooms, fresh		1.02	1.05	0.89	0.92	0.97	0.95	27
Tomatoes, fresh		2.49	4.11	4.82	3.09	3.63	3.08	45
Miiscellaneous fresh vegetables		1.22	1.67	1.98	1.53	1.60	1.48	21
Total other fresh vegetables		15.73	15.99	16.34	16.71	16.19	14.67	75
Tomatoes, canned or bottled		1.60	1.56	1.38	1.45	1.50	1.50	19
Canned peas		1.61	1.71	1.41	1.47	1.55	1.54	19
Canned beans		4.84	4.32	3.98	4.33	4.37	4.37	40
Canned vegetables, other than pulses, potaoes or tomatoes		1.02	1.16	1.05	1.03	1.06	1.06	15
Dried pulses, other than air-dried		0.29	0.19	0.17	0.31	0.24	0.24	5
Air-dried vegetables		0.01	–	–	0.01	–	–	...
Vegetable juices	(fl oz)	0.17	0.25	0.20	0.19	0.20	0.20	4
Chips, excluding frozen		0.69	0.64	0.84	0.59	0.69	0.69	17
Instant potato		0.05	0.06	0.04	0.04	0.05	0.05	1
Canned potato		0.19	0.28	0.22	0.17	0.22	0.22	2
Crisps and other potato products, not frozen		1.21	1.24	1.18	1.29	1.23	1.23	34
Other vegetable products		0.76	1.15	1.13	0.91	0.99	0.98	21

Table 1 *continued*

	Consumption					Purchases	Percentage of all households purchasing each type of food during Survey week
	Jan/ March	April/ June	July/ Sept	Oct/ Dec	Yearly average	Yearly average	
VEGETABLES continued							
Frozen peas	2.02	1.73	1.57	1.72	1.76	1.76	14
Frozen beans	0.49	0.53	0.30	0.29	0.40	0.40	4
Frozen chips and other frozen convenience potato products	2.75	2.71	2.40	2.45	2.58	2.58	15
All frozen vegetables and frozen vegetable products, not specified elsewhere	2.05	1.91	1.67	1.59	1.80	1.80	14
Total processed vegetables	**19.75**	**19.44**	**17.54**	**17.84**	**18.64**	**18.62**	**80**
Total vegetables	**80.10**	**79.63**	**76.70**	**82.78**	**79.79**	**74.89**	**94**
FRUIT :							
Fresh							
Oranges	4.01	3.59	1.85	1.85	2.82	2.82	22
Other citrus fruit	2.16	1.31	0.82	3.16	1.86	1.86	18
Apples	7.87	7.24	6.14	7.11	7.09	6.55	49
Pears	1.47	1.17	1.15	1.56	1.34	1.32	15
Stone fruit	0.23	0.79	3.12	0.26	1.10	1.08	11
Grapes	0.69	0.93	1.00	0.73	0.83	0.82	12
Soft fruit, other than grapes	0.21	1.11	1.35	0.13	0.70	0.46	5
Bananas	3.99	4.75	4.47	4.36	4.39	4.38	43
Rhubarb	0.14	0.45	0.13	0.02	0.18	0.06	1
Other fresh fruit	0.49	0.98	2.04	0.50	1.00	0.99	8
Total fresh fruit	**21.26**	**22.32**	**22.07**	**19.68**	**21.33**	**20.32**	**73**
Canned peaches, pears and pineapples	0.89	1.03	0.95	1.00	0.97	0.97	13
Other canned or bottled fruit	0.94	0.77	0.79	0.94	0.86	0.86	11
Dried fruit and dried fruit products	0.52	0.50	0.56	1.33	0.73	0.73	9
Frozen fruit and frozen fruit products	0.02	0.02	0.02	0.06	0.03	0.03	...
Nuts and nut products	0.43	0.47	0.37	0.87	0.54	0.53	12
Fruit juices (fl oz)	6.80	7.48	7.14	7.00	7.11	7.10	27
Total other fruit and fruit products	**9.60**	**10.28**	**9.84**	**11.19**	**10.23**	**10.22**	**48**
Total fruit	**30.86**	**32.60**	**31.91**	**30.87**	**31.56**	**30.54**	**80**
CEREALS :							
White bread, large loaves, unsliced	3.78	3.53	3.49	3.50	3.57	3.56	18
White bread, large loaves, sliced	9.51	9.78	9.91	10.08	9.82	9.81	40
White bread, small loaves, unsliced	0.95	0.87	1.04	0.99	0.96	0.96	11
White bread, small loaves, sliced	0.42	0.30	0.38	0.54	0.41	0.41	5
Brown bread	3.54	3.90	3.25	3.13	3.45	3.45	25
Wholewheat and wholemeal bread	4.03	4.09	3.61	3.55	3.82	3.82	24
Other bread[a]	6.09	6.13	6.31	5.65	6.04	6.04	51
Total bread	**28.31**	**28.61**	**27.98**	**27.45**	**28.09**	**28.06**	**91**
Flour	3.83	2.73	2.79	3.43	3.19	3.19	13
Buns, scones and teacakes	1.37	1.29	0.78	1.28	1.18	1.18	23
Cakes and pastries	2.12	2.50	2.33	2.94	2.47	2.47	41
Crispbread	0.21	0.20	0.21	0.14	0.19	0.19	6
Biscuits, other than chocolate biscuits	3.43	3.62	3.48	3.88	3.60	3.60	50
Chocolate biscuits	1.45	1.47	1.38	1.56	1.47	1.46	33
Oatmeal and oat products	0.74	0.46	0.39	0.48	0.52	0.52	8
Breakfast cereals	4.26	4.66	4.51	4.47	4.47	4.47	42
Canned milk puddings	0.93	0.86	0.62	0.91	0.83	0.83	9
Other puddings	0.15	0.15	0.14	0.33	0.19	0.19	4
Rice	1.17	1.07	0.85	0.94	1.01	1.01	8
Cereal-based invalid foods (including 'slimming' foods)	–	–	0.01	–	0.01	0.01	...
Infant cereal foods	0.07	0.06	0.07	0.12	0.08	0.08	2
Frozen convenience cereal foods[a]	1.22	1.31	1.24	1.07	1.21	1.21	16
Cereal convenience foods, including canned, not specified elsewhere[a]	2.63	2.41	2.50	2.52	2.52	2.51	38
Other cereal foods	0.80	0.86	0.66	0.74	0.77	0.77	10
Total cereals	**52.69**	**52.28**	**49.95**	**52.26**	**51.79**	**51.74**	**96**

Table 1 *continued*

		Consumption					Purchases	Percentage of all households purchasing each type of food during Survey week
		Jan/ March	April/ June	July/ Sept	Oct/ Dec	Yearly average	Yearly average	
BEVERAGES :								
Tea		1.49	1.45	1.53	1.60	1.52	1.52	37
Coffee, bean and ground		0.14	0.18	0.11	0.15	0.14	0.14	3
Coffee, instant		0.54	0.46	0.42	0.49	0.48	0.48	23
Coffee, essences	(fl oz)	–	0.01	–	0.01	0.01	0.01	...
Cocoa and drinking chocolate		0.18	0.14	0.14	0.19	0.16	0.16	4
Branded food drinks		0.20	0.15	0.14	0.13	0.16	0.16	3
Total beverages		**2.56**	**2.39**	**2.34**	**2.57**	**2.47**	**2.46**	**53**
MISCELLANEOUS								
Mineral water	(fl oz)	1.75	1.84	2.37	1.90	1.96	1.96	5
Baby foods, canned or bottled		0.19	0.32	0.41	0.30	0.30	0.30	2
Soups, canned		2.93	2.00	1.93	2.77	2.41	2.41	21
Soups, dehydrated and powdered		0.13	0.11	0.08	0.14	0.11	0.11	7
Accelerated freeze-dried foods (excluding coffee)		–	–	–	–	–	–	–
Spreads and dressings		0.43	0.79	0.78	0.48	0.62	0.62	12
Pickles and sauces		2.33	2.35	2.35	2.45	2.37	2.37	30
Meat and yeats extracts		0.18	0.14	0.14	0.15	0.15	0.15	10
Table jellies, squares and crystals		0.21	0.19	0.18	0.16	0.18	0.18	6
Ice-cream, mousse	(fl oz)	2.74	3.38	4.12	3.00	3.31	3.31	19
All frozen convenience foods, not specified elsewhere		–	0.01	–	–	–	–	...
Salt		0.36	0.45	0.39	0.47	0.42	0.42	4
Novel protein foods		0.02	0.01	0.01	0.01	0.01	0.01	...

(a) These foods are given in greater detail in this table under 'Supplementary classifications'.

Table 1 *continued*

Supplementary classifications[b]		Consumption					Purchases	Percentage of all households purchasing each type of food during Survey week
		Jan/ March	April/ June	July/ Sept	Oct/ Dec	Yearly average	Yearly average	
MILK AND CREAM :								
Liquid wholemilk, full price								
UHT	(pt)	0.02	0.02	0.02	0.02	0.02	0.02	2
sterilised	(pt)	0.11	0.07	0.09	0.12	0.10	0.10	5
other	(pt)	2.14	2.04	1.95	1.90	2.01	1.95	64
Total liquid wholemilk, full price	(pt)	**2.26**	**2.13**	**2.05**	**2.04**	**2.12**	**2.07**	**67**
Skimmed milks:								
fully skimmed	(pt)	0.33	0.35	0.35	0.33	0.34	0.34	16
semi and other skimmed	(pt)	0.87	0.90	0.84	1.03	0.91	0.91	33
Total skimmed milks	(pt)	**1.20**	**1.25**	**1.18**	**1.36**	**1.25**	**1.25**	**44**
CHEESE :								
Natural hard:								
Cheddar and Cheddar type		2.44	2.55	2.48	2.59	2.51	2.51	44
other UK varieties or foreign equivalents		0.49	0.48	0.56	0.58	0.53	0.53	12
Edam and other continental		0.21	0.21	0.28	0.24	0.24	0.24	7
Natural soft		0.40	0.54	0.40	0.35	0.42	0.42	12
Total natural cheese		**3.55**	**3.78**	**3.71**	**3.75**	**3.70**	**3.69**	**59**
CARCASE MEAT :								
Beef: joints (including sides) on the bone		0.08	0.66	0.12	0.15	0.25	0.25	1
joints, boned		1.58	1.18	1.17	1.57	1.37	1.36	10
steak, less expensive varieties		1.49	0.83	0.87	1.33	1.13	1.13	15
steak, more expensive varieties		0.78	0.69	0.56	0.65	0.67	0.66	10
minced		2.10	1.68	1.65	1.64	1.77	1.76	24
other, and veal		0.03	0.09	0.03	0.03	0.05	0.05	1
Total beef and veal		**6.06**	**5.13**	**4.40**	**5.37**	**5.24**	**5.21**	**43**
Mutton		0.01	0.01	0.01	0.02	0.01	0.01	...
Lamb: joints (including sides)		1.56	1.72	1.99	1.83	1.77	1.76	9
chops (including cutlets and fillets)		0.81	0.77	1.00	0.92	0.87	0.87	12
all other		0.35	0.25	0.17	0.28	0.26	0.26	3
Total mutton and lamb		**2.72**	**2.75**	**3.16**	**3.04**	**2.92**	**2.90**	**21**
Pork: joints (including sides)		1.20	1.22	0.67	0.95	1.01	1.00	6
chops		1.33	1.14	1.19	1.16	1.20	1.20	16
fillets and steaks		0.27	0.35	0.29	0.25	0.29	0.29	4
all other		0.41	0.59	0.40	0.45	0.46	0.46	5
Total pork		**3.21**	**3.30**	**2.56**	**2.80**	**2.97**	**2.95**	**27**
OTHER MEAT AND MEAT PRODUCTS								
Liver: ox		0.07	0.05	0.01	0.06	0.05	0.05	1
lambs		0.27	0.19	0.17	0.23	0.22	0.22	5
pigs		0.18	0.10	0.10	0.05	0.11	0.11	2
other		0.01	0.02	—	0.02	0.01	0.01	...
Total liver		**0.52**	**0.37**	**0.29**	**0.36**	**0.38**	**0.38**	**8**
Bacon and ham, uncooked:								
joints (including sides and steaks cut from joint)		0.78	0.85	0.72	0.84	0.80	0.80	9
rashers, vacuum-packed		0.70	0.69	0.72	0.71	0.70	0.70	15
rashers, not vacuum-packed		1.62	1.50	1.40	1.57	1.52	1.52	28
Total bacon and ham, uncooked		**3.10**	**3.03**	**2.84**	**3.12**	**3.02**	**3.02**	**46**
Poultry, uncooked, including frozen:								
chicken, other than broilers		1.27	1.41	1.32	1.22	1.31	1.31	4
turkey		0.60	1.29	0.46	1.21	0.89	0.89	5
all other		0.07	0.12	0.06	0.14	0.10	0.10	...
Total poultry, uncooked, other than broilers		**1.95**	**2.83**	**1.85**	**2.58**	**2.30**	**2.30**	**10**

Table 1 *continued*

Supplementary classifications[b]	Consumption					Purchases	Percentage of all households purchasing each type of food during Survey week
	Jan/ March	April/ June	July/ Sept	Oct/ Dec	Yearly average	Yearly average	
OTHER MEAT AND MEAT PRODUCTS continued							
Meat pies and sausage rolls, ready-to-eat:							
meat pies	0.36	0.49	0.38	0.34	0.39	0.39	9
sausage rolls	0.16	0.17	0.15	0.23	0.18	0.18	5
Total meat pies and sausage rolls, ready-to-eat	**0.52**	**0.65**	**0.53**	**0.57**	**0.57**	**0.57**	**14**
Frozen convenience meats or frozen convenience meat products							
frozen burgers	0.66	0.72	0.77	0.76	0.73	0.73	10
other	1.34	1.48	1.30	1.48	1.40	1.40	16
Total frozen convenience meats or frozen convenience meat products	**2.00**	**2.21**	**2.06**	**2.23**	**2.13**	**2.13**	**23**
Other meat products							
delicatessen-type sausages	0.23	0.34	0.29	0.26	0.28	0.28	10
meat pastes and spreads	0.07	0.08	0.04	0.07	0.06	0.06	5
meat pies, pasties and puddings	0.99	0.98	1.08	1.11	1.04	1.04	19
ready meals	1.07	0.86	0.85	0.93	0.93	0.93	12
other meat products, not specified elsewhere	0.58	0.92	0.74	0.66	0.73	0.73	14
Total other meat products	**2.95**	**3.18**	**3.02**	**3.02**	**3.04**	**3.04**	**43**
FATS :							
Butter: New Zealand	0.51	0.62	0.40	0.48	0.50	0.50	8
Danish	0.35	0.29	0.29	0.32	0.31	0.31	5
UK	0.32	0.32	0.28	0.32	0.31	0.31	5
other	0.43	0.37	0.50	0.65	0.49	0.48	8
Total butter	**1.61**	**1.60**	**1.46**	**1.77**	**1.61**	**1.60**	**25**
Margarine: soft	2.94	3.03	2.92	3.03	2.98	2.98	31
other	0.30	0.21	0.11	0.24	0.21	0.21	3
Total margarine	**3.24**	**3.23**	**3.03**	**3.27**	**3.19**	**3.19**	**33**
Other fats:							
reduced fat spreads	0.76	0.70	0.63	0.64	0.68	0.68	10
low fat spreads	0.85	0.92	0.87	0.97	0.90	0.90	13
other fats	0.26	0.27	0.28	0.29	0.28	0.28	6
Total other fats	**1.87**	**1.89**	**1.78**	**1.91**	**1.86**	**1.86**	**26**
CEREALS:							
Other bread:							
rolls (excluding starch reduced rolls)	2.79	2.82	3.05	2.51	2.80	2.79	34
malt bread and fruit bread	0.16	0.18	0.19	0.19	0.18	0.18	4
Vienna bread and French bread	0.42	0.54	0.54	0.61	0.53	0.53	8
starch reduced bread and rolls	0.15	0.13	0.21	0.15	0.16	0.16	2
other	2.57	2.46	2.32	2.19	2.38	2.38	19
Total other bread	**6.09**	**6.13**	**6.31**	**5.65**	**6.04**	**6.04**	**51**
Frozen convenience cereal foods:							
cakes and pastires	0.47	0.46	0.41	0.52	0.46	0.46	6
other frozen convenience cereal foods	0.75	0.85	0.84	0.55	0.75	0.74	11
Total frozen convenience cereal foods	**1.22**	**1.31**	**1.24**	**1.07**	**1.21**	**1.21**	**16**
Cereal convenience foods, including canned, not specified elsewhere:							
canned pasta	1.25	1.11	1.12	1.17	1.16	1.16	14
pizza	0.45	0.57	0.57	0.50	0.52	0.52	8
cake, pudding and dessert mixes	0.44	0.30	0.37	0.37	0.37	0.37	11
other cereal convenience foods	0.49	0.43	0.45	0.48	0.46	0.46	19
Total cereal convenience foods, including canned, not specified elsewhere	**2.63**	**2.41**	**2.50**	**2.52**	**2.52**	**2.51**	**38**

(b) Supplementary data for certain foods in greater detail than shown elsewhere in the table; the totals for each main food are repeated for ease of reference.

Table 2
Household food prices for
individual foods, 1988-1990

pence per lb [a]

	Average prices paid		
	1988	1989	1990
MILK AND CREAM:			
Liquid wholemilk, full price	25.78	27.69	29.87
Condensed milk	23.56	26.50	28.43
Dried milk, branded	35.82	36.92	39.86
Instant miilk	15.69	18.81	19.56
Yoghurt	80.58	87.17	96.59
Other milk	27.13	29.46	31.36
Cream	145.74	148.85	162.11
CHEESE:			
Natural	146.41	155.46	163.36
Processed	167.32	179.86	195.87
MEAT AND MEAT PRODUCTS:			
Carcase meat			
Beef and veal	179.20	198.46	196.15
Mutton and lamb	143.47	147.36	158.22
Pork	127.20	142.39	157.52
Other meat and meat products			
Liver	88.10	92.85	100.41
Offals, other than liver	83.33	94.85	111.15
Bacon and ham, uncooked	140.50	157.00	179.80
Bacon and ham, cooked, including canned	199.87	219.33	253.88
Cooked poultry, not purchased in cans	196.04	206.55	233.55
Corned meat	112.09	125.86	145.40
Other cooked meat, not purchased in cans	205.84	209.92	241.39
Other canned meat and canned meat products	74.52	81.65	87.84
Broiler chicken, uncooked, including frozen	91.85	99.45	113.23
Other poultry, uncooked, including frozen	84.95	89.37	95.97
Rabbit and other meat	87.80	113.85	138.34
Sausages, uncooked, pork	91.74	97.38	108.28
Sausages, uncooked, beef	79.87	86.17	93.06
Meat pies and sausage rolls, ready-to-eat	117.58	136.81	152.11
Frozen convenience meats or frozen convenience meat products	126.04	138.94	155.65
Other meat products	178.41	204.99	227.75
FISH:			
White, filleted, fresh	188.57	195.99	220.12
White, unfilleted, fresh	153.14	159.46	163.06
White, uncooked, frozen	166.33	167.45	188.02
Herrings, filleted, fresh	92.44	94.17	126.98
Herrings, unfilleted, fresh	82.19	75.02	98.26
Fat, fresh, other than herrings	202.17	205.04	240.29
White, processed	183.17	195.59	223.30
Fat, processed, filleted	184.13	204.41	211.08
Fat, processed, unfilleted	142.97	100.62	135.32
Shellfish	344.62	391.18	371.44
Cooked fish	234.23	289.66	328.40
Canned salmon	265.12	342.11	288.63
Other canned or bottled fish	119.92	126.80	124.84
Fish products, not frozen	249.57	271.55	276.05
Frozen convenience fish products	141.38	144.65	166.19
EGGS	7.48	8.03	9.21
FATS:			
Butter	96.07	107.81	109.79
Margarine	42.67	45.64	49.96
Lard and compound cooking fat	31.57	34.26	35.94
Vegetable and salad oils	42.04	45.77	49.11
Other fats	72.83	76.72	82.01
SUGAR AND PRESERVES:			
Sugar	26.07	27.46	29.40
Jams, jellies and fruit curds	56.69	60.07	65.80
Marmalade	51.18	55.96	63.20

Table 2 *continued*

	Average prices paid		
	1988	1989	1990
SUGAR AND PRESERVES *continued*			
Syrup, treacle	46.64	49.04	59.61
Honey	82.44	85.27	92.92
VEGETABLES:			
Old potatoes			
January-August			
not prepacked	8.81	8.89	12.34
prepacked	12.40	12.37	16.69
New potatoes			
January-August			
not prepacked	14.61	18.25	16.76
prepacked	15.90	17.60	17.65
Potatoes			
September-December			
not prepacked	7.95	10.39	9.94
prepacked	10.58	14.07	13.04
Fresh			
Cabbages	23.77	24.86	27.33
Brussels sprouts	25.38	28.16	31.70
Cauliflowers	28.31	30.11	33.19
Leafy salads	61.80	65.07	70.14
Peas	72.70	69.36	88.94
Beans	61.49	68.67	77.23
Other green vegetables	80.51	80.63	85.29
Carrots	21.84	21.46	25.70
Turnips and swedes	18.16	19.76	23.90
Other root vegetables	36.04	40.05	45.97
Onions, shallots, leeks	29.26	30.47	35.54
Cucumbers	53.61	57.15	62.11
Mushrooms	109.47	111.21	117.93
Tomatoes	57.23	58.19	63.56
Miscellaneous fresh vegetables	67.52	70.20	79.16
Processed			
Tomatoes, canned or bottled	25.14	30.00	33.06
Canned peas	28.59	30.89	34.12
Canned beans	26.63	29.90	30.72
Canned vegetables, othet than pulses, potatoes or tomatoes	43.71	47.46	52.15
Dricd pulcoc, other than air-dried	54.65	52.67	62.76
Air-dried vegetables	388.69	318.65	250.97
Vegetables juices	64.67	67.05	81.09
Chips, excuding frozen	137.18	149.05	156.36
Instant potato	101.71	115.31	114.07
Canned potato	34.61	35.97	38.87
Crisps and other potato products, not frozen	174.64	187.38	205.23
Other vegetable products	126.20	135.06	151.90
Frozen peas	44.54	46.24	48.37
Frozen beans	49.63	48.75	49.07
Frozen chips and other frozen convenience potato products	34.85	36.17	43.67
All frozen vegetable and frozen vegetable products, not specified elsewhere	55.87	59.24	64.74
FRUIT:			
Fresh			
Oranges	32.80	34.03	38.00
Other citrus fruit	38.81	40.20	47.69
Apples	35.55	36.79	44.99
Pears	35.29	42.86	49.93
Stone fruit	60.41	65.50	73.83
Grapes	79.34	86.80	94.65
Soft fruit, other than grapes	88.27	97.15	108.10
Bananas	45.74	46.65	49.69

Table 2 *continued*

	Average prices paid		
	1988	1989	1990
FRUIT *continued*			
Rhubarb	34.09	33.95	33.67
Other fresh fruit	52.90	59.42	59.29
Canned peaches, pears and pineapples	40.70	42.15	44.10
Other canned or bottled fruit	49.64	51.73	55.45
Dried fruit and dried fruit products	69.75	73.42	84.35
Frozen fruits and frozen fruit products	104.13	105.31	126.17
Nuts and nut products	130.01	133.72	152.94
Fruit juices	40.91	42.71	48.56
CEREALS:			
White bread, large loaves, unsliced	30.02	30.81	32.52
White bread, large loaves, sliced	25.55	26.55	27.78
White bread, small loaves, unsliced	43.37	45.52	47.70
White bread, small loaves, sliced	42.78	44.88	47.43
Brown bread	35.16	36.86	38.51
Wholewheat and wholemeal bread	34.18	35.77	37.47
Other bread	50.64	55.44	60.80
Flour	16.26	17.76	17.75
Buns, scones and teacakes	76.63	83.43	87.86
Cakes and pastries	125.49	134.65	145.82
Crispbread	76.75	85.66	96.36
Biscuits, other than chocoloate	68.47	71.94	77.51
Chocolate biscuits	129.45	138.38	144.28
Oatmeal and oat products	70.67	63.52	68.21
Breakfast cereals	80.19	87.52	94.77
Canned milk puddings	36.03	39.29	41.93
Other puddings	126.25	134.90	144.57
Rice	52.95	53.19	58.57
Cereal-based invalid foods (including 'slimming' foods)	430.17	252.76	251.55
Infant cereal foods	243.67	255.05	278.14
Frozen convenience cereal foods	121.66	131.35	140.08
Cereal convenience foods, including canned, not specified elsewhere	92.75	102.95	125.59
Other cereal foods	51.72	53.43	62.70
BEVERAGES:			
Tea	168.56	180.54	211.63
Coffee, bean and ground	266.43	262.13	261.25
Coffee, instant	585.31	626.39	582.06
Coffee, essences	221.11	218.39	231.34
Cocoa and drinking chocolate	155.01	153.30	167.23
Branded food drinks	137.65	143.81	161.69
MISCELLANEOUS:			
Mineral water	21.73	20.94	21.44
Baby foods, canned or bottled	81.26	84.34	101.46
Soups, canned	33.00	35.43	38.34
Soups, dehydrated and powdered	243.56	280.60	299.32
Accelerated freeze-dried foods (excluding coffee)	–	–	–
Spreads and dressings	83.22	85.10	91.86
Pickles and sauces	63.51	69.01	76.48
Meat and yeast extracts	269.72	279.07	307.10
Table jellies, squares and crystals	67.49	71.80	83.63
Ice-cream, mousse	46.43	52.26	56.87
All frozen convenience foods, not specified elsewhere	104.20	194.23	74.33
Salt	18.57	21.02	22.93
Novel protein foods	148.33	98.47	212.03

(a) Pence per lb, except per pint of milk, yoghurt, cream, vegetable and salad oils, vegetable juices, fruit juices, coffee essence; per equivalent pint of condensed, dried and instant milk; per one-tenth gallon of ice-cream; per egg.

Table 3

Soft drinks: purchases and expenditure: annual averages, 1990

per person per week

	Concentrated		Unconcentrated		Low-calorie		All soft drinks	
	Purchase quantity	Expenditure	Purchase quantity	Expenditure	Purchase quantity	Expenditure	Purchase quantity	(a) Energy
	fl oz	pence	fl oz	pence	fl oz	pence	equivalent fl oz[(b)]	kcal
All households	4.07	8.97	12.82	17.58	4.55	6.12	37.72	36
Analysis by region								
Scotland	4.19	9.23	17.26	23.03	5.94	7.99	44.15	42
Wales	3.25	6.89	11.80	15.05	3.88	5.58	31.93	31
England	4.12	9.08	12.44	17.21	4.45	5.97	37.49	35
North	3.85	8.22	12.66	15.72	3.42	4.33	35.33	34
Yorkshire and Humberside	3.74	7.63	11.56	14.36	4.90	5.55	35.16	33
North West	3.33	7.75	11.27	15.18	3.88	5.05	31.80	30
East Midlands	4.22	9.07	13.39	18.11	3.96	4.93	38.45	37
West Midlands	4.27	9.38	14.40	17.53	3.47	4.68	39.22	39
South West	4.77	10.09	11.29	15.38	4.46	5.79	39.60	37
South East[(c)]/East Anglia	4.29	9.71	12.62	19.22	5.13	7.37	39.20	37
Analysis by type of area								
Greater London	3.85	8.48	13.58	21.65	5.38	7.86	38.21	36
Metropolitan districts and Central Clydeside Conurbation	3.73	8.11	13.69	17.05	4.45	5.55	36.79	35
Non-metropolitan districts with electorate per acre of:								
7 or more	4.31	9.91	14.08	18.81	4.20	6.16	39.83	38
3 but less than 7	4.58	9.85	11.45	15.70	4.47	5.71	38.82	36
0.5 but less than 3	4.01	8.95	13.02	17.82	4.62	6.51	37.69	36
Less than 0.5	4.39	9.64	11.29	16.19	4.28	5.56	37.52	35
Analysis by income group								
A1	3.73	8.18	13.22	20.90	6.55	9.33	38.42	35
A2	3.32	7.57	13.18	21.51	5.85	8.36	35.63	33
All A	3.46	7.80	13.22	21.22	6.13	8.71	36.65	34
B	4.69	10.48	13.48	19.27	5.71	7.72	42.64	40
C	4.31	9.35	14.35	18.07	4.37	5.73	40.27	39
D	3.95	8.60	17.39	20.30	2.43	3.13	39.57	41
E1	2.31	5.54	5.80	9.32	1.59	2.42	18.94	18
E2	3.28	6.87	10.51	14.22	2.77	3.72	29.68	29
OAP	2.36	4.98	4.89	6.62	2.15	2.48	18.84	17

Analysis by household composition

Number of adults	Number of children								
1	0	2.81	6.82	7.36	11.25	2.90	4.52	24.31	23
1	1 or more	4.96	10.00	16.72	22.32	4.23	5.63	45.75	45
2	0	2.67	5.86	9.74	14.19	4.86	6.70	27.95	25
2	1	4.39	9.92	15.72	21.57	5.81	8.06	43.48	41
2	2	6.02	13.32	15.87	21.48	5.30	6.73	51.27	49
2	3	5.91	12.77	13.63	17.60	4.10	5.48	47.28	45
2	4 or more	6.43	12.41	18.05	22.04	2.63	3.38	52.83	53
3	0	2.64	5.90	10.74	14.62	3.95	5.49	27.89	26
3 or more	1 or 2	4.13	8.88	16.04	21.29	4.05	5.29	40.74	40
3 or more	3 or more	5.70	14.79	12.46	14.72	1.12	1.72	42.08	42
4 or more	0	2.53	5.39	11.28	15.75	5.62	6.86	29.55	27

(a) Per person per day.

(b) Converted to unconcentrated equivalent.

(c) Including Greater London, for which separate results are shown in the analysis according to type of area.

Table 4

Meals eaten outside the home, 1990

per person per week

| | Meals not from the household supply | | Net balance[a] | |
	Mid-day meals	All meals out	Persons	Visitors
All households	1.93	3.76	0.85	0.05
Analysis by region				
Scotland	1.80	3.49	0.87	0.05
Wales	1.85	3.35	0.86	0.04
England	1.95	3.82	0.85	0.05
North	2.15	3.71	0.85	0.05
Yorkshire and Humberside	2.01	3.78	0.86	0.05
North West	2.17	3.77	0.85	0.04
East Midlands	1.69	3.05	0.88	0.05
West Midlands	1.69	3.08	0.88	0.05
South West	1.56	3.20	0.87	0.05
South East/East Anglia	2.04	4.37	0.83	0.05
Analysis by income group				
A1	2.58	5.11	0.79	0.07
A2	2.40	4.64	0.81	0.06
B	2.16	4.15	0.84	0.05
C	2.04	3.83	0.85	0.04
D	1.76	3.16	0.88	0.05
E1	1.09	2.83	0.89	0.06
E2	1.31	2.75	0.90	0.05
OAP (households containing one adult)	1.03	2.45	0.91	0.06
OAP (households containing one male and one female)	0.55	1.45	0.95	0.03
OAP ("other" households)	1.10	2.74	0.90	0.04
OAP (all)	0.81	2.01	0.93	0.04
Analysis by household composition				
Number of adults / Number of children				
1 / 0	1.75	4.22	0.85	0.08
1 / 1 or more	2.69	4.84	0.81	0.06
2 / 0	1.61	3.88	0.87	0.06
2 / 1	2.14	4.13	0.84	0.05
2 / 2	2.02	3.38	0.86	0.03
2 / 3	2.02	3.05	0.87	0.03
2 / 4 or more	1.88	2.50	0.88	0.03
3 / 0	1.81	4.00	0.85	0.05
3 or more / 1 or 2	2.16	3.67	0.84	0.04
3 or more / 3 or more	2.35	2.94	0.84	0.03
4 or more / 0	2.13	4.12	0.83	0.04
Analysis by age of housewife				
Under 25 years	2.39	6.03	0.80	0.05
25-34 years	2.20	4.17	0.83	0.04
35-44 years	2.27	3.85	0.84	0.04
45-54 years	2.00	3.91	0.85	0.06
55-64 years	1.35	3.05	0.89	0.07
65-74 years	0.88	2.15	0.92	0.05
75 and over	0.93	2.03	0.92	0.03
Analysis by housing tenure				
Unfurnished: council	1.76	3.36	0.87	0.04
other, rented	1.81	3.54	0.86	0.04
Furnished, rented	2.63	6.03	0.77	0.07
Rent free	1.38	2.95	0.88	0.05
Owned outright	1.43	3.06	0.88	0.06
Owned with mortgage	2.19	4.14	0.84	0.05
Analysis by ownership of deep-freezer				
Households owning a deep-freezer	1.81	3.57	0.86	0.05
Households not owning a deep-freezer	1.76	3.71	0.86	0.04

(a) See Glossary.

Table 5

Average number of mid-day meals per week per child aged 5-14 years, 1990

	Meals not from the household supply		Meals from the household supply	
	School meals	Other meals out	Packed meals	Other
All households	2.08	0.37	1.60	2.95
Analysis by region				
Scotland	2.23	0.33	0.78	3.66
Wales	2.79	0.40	0.69	3.12
England	2.01	0.37	1.75	2.87
North	2.82	0.48	0.82	2.88
Yorkshire and Humberside	2.26	0.41	1.18	3.15
North West	2.32	0.33	1.24	3.11
East Midlands	2.10	0.23	1.86	2.81
West Midlands	2.09	0.33	1.60	2.99
South West	1.34	0.40	2.50	2.76
South East/East Anglia	1.77	0.38	2.15	2.70
Analysis by income group				
A1	1.71	0.35	2.49	2.45
A2	1.77	0.46	2.16	2.61
B	1.83	0.40	1.95	2.82
C	2.13	0.36	1.46	3.05
D	3.12	0.35	0.35	3.18
E1	2.17	0.25	1.04	3.54
E2	2.79	0.16	0.31	3.74
OAP (all)	(a)	(a)	(a)	(a)
Analysis by household composition				

Number of adults	Number of children				
1	1 or more	2.92	0.21	0.61	3.26
2	1	2.36	0.58	1.70	2.36
2	2	1.89	0.36	1.86	2.89
2	3	1.91	0.34	1.68	3.07
2	4 or more	1.95	0.22	1.47	3.36
3 or more	1 or 2	2.02	0.60	1.61	2.77
3 or more	3 or more	2.61	0.34	0.93	3.12

	School meals	Other meals out	Packed meals	Other
Analysis by age of housewife				
Under 25 years	2.50	0.21	0.50	3.79
25-34 years	2.04	0.28	1.34	3.34
35-44 years	2.08	0.41	1.81	2.70
45-54 years	2.27	0.46	1.57	2.70
55-64 years	1.24	0.53	1.35	3.88
65-74 years	(a)	(a)	(a)	(a)
75 and over	(a)	(a)	(a)	(a)
Analysis by housing tenure				
Unfurnished: council	2.46	0.33	0.84	3.37
other, rented	2.56	0.29	0.85	3.30
Furnished, rented	(a)	(a)	(a)	(a)
Rent free	(a)	(a)	(a)	(a)
Owned outright	2.32	0.52	1.32	2.84
Owned with mortgage	1.89	0.37	1.90	2.84
Analysis by ownership of deep-freezer				
Households owning a deep-freezer	2.05	0.37	1.63	2.95
Households not owning a deep-freezer	2.37	0.27	1.16	3.20

(a) Estimates are not shown because these household groups contain samples of fewer than 20 children aged 5-14 years.

Table 6
Household food consumption by main food groups, according to income group for 1990

ounces per person per week

		Income groups								
		Gross weekly income of head of household								
		Households with one or more earners						Households without an earner		OAP
		£645 and over	£475 and under £645	£475 and over	£250 and under £475	£125 and under £250	Less than £125	£125 or more	Less than £125	
		A1	A2	All A	B	C	D	E1	E2	
MILK AND CREAM:										
Liquid wholemilk, full price	(pt)	1.74	1.60	1.65	1.92	2.22	2.41	2.46	2.34	2.89
Welfare and school milk	(pt)	0.02	0.01	0.02	0.01	0.02	0.20	...	0.23	...
Condensed milk	(pt)	0.03	0.03	0.03	0.04	0.04	0.03	0.08	0.09	0.08
Dried and other milk	(pt or eq pt)	1.80	2.05	1.95	1.69	1.45	1.21	2.14	1.32	1.32
Cream	(pt)	0.04	0.04	0.04	0.03	0.02	0.02	0.05	0.02	0.02
Total milk and cream	(pt or eq pt)	**3.63**	**3.72**	**3.68**	**3.70**	**3.74**	**3.87**	**4.72**	**4.00**	**4.31**
CHEESE:										
Natural		4.57	4.47	4.50	3.85	3.43	3.25	4.78	3.23	3.27
Processed		0.24	0.30	0.28	0.32	0.32	0.21	0.27	0.30	0.22
Total cheese		**4.81**	**4.77**	**4.78**	**4.17**	**3.75**	**3.46**	**5.05**	**3.53**	**3.50**
MEAT:										
Beef and veal		4.94	4.52	4.70	5.58	5.10	4.68	6.39	4.93	5.22
Mutton and lamb		3.31	2.91	3.08	2.66	2.79	2.94	4.27	3.35	3.63
Pork		3.38	2.17	2.67	3.05	3.07	2.86	3.06	2.84	2.83
Total carcase meat		11.64	9.60	10.45	11.29	10.96	10.48	13.73	11.11	11.67
Bacon and ham, uncooked		2.68	2.29	2.44	2.77	3.08	3.00	3.88	3.61	3.85
Poultry, uncooked		8.09	8.07	8.04	7.86	7.08	6.74	9.28	6.80	6.00
Other meat and meat products		10.16	10.43	10.37	12.49	13.44	13.59	11.48	12.59	11.78
Total meat		**32.58**	**30.40**	**31.29**	**34.41**	**34.55**	**33.80**	**38.36**	**34.10**	**33.31**
FISH:										
Fresh		1.26	1.06	1.13	0.99	0.84	0.90	3.58	1.31	1.96
Processed and shell		0.74	0.50	0.60	0.50	0.40	0.40	1.39	0.53	0.58
Prepared, including fish products		2.07	1.67	1.82	1.75	1.77	1.70	1.62	1.75	1.87
Frozen, including fish products		1.37	1.25	1.30	1.60	1.51	1.67	2.20	1.95	2.24
Total fish		**5.44**	**4.47**	**4.87**	**4.82**	**4.54**	**4.67**	**8.80**	**5.69**	**6.65**
EGGS	(no)	1.98	1.84	1.90	1.85	2.27	2.61	2.78	2.65	3.13
(Eggs purchased)	(no)	1.86	1.76	1.81	1.74	2.18	2.55	2.74	2.59	3.11
FATS:										
Butter		1.89	1.56	1.67	1.39	1.38	1.60	2.60	1.95	2.66
Margarine		2.12	2.61	2.42	2.81	3.11	3.56	3.42	4.40	4.79
Lard and compound cooking fat		0.32	0.37	0.35	0.61	0.89	1.13	0.79	1.22	1.42
Low-fat and dairy spreads		1.28	1.69	1.52	1.67	1.59	1.26	1.71	1.49	1.69
Other fats		1.57	1.65	1.64	1.94	1.80	1.27	1.81	1.76	1.79
Total fats		**7.18**	**7.88**	**7.60**	**8.41**	**8.77**	**8.81**	**10.33**	**10.82**	**12.34**
SUGAR AND PRESERVES:										
Sugar		3.14	4.02	3.67	4.71	6.30	7.60	8.65	8.20	10.49
Honey, preserves, syrup and treacle		1.85	1.74	1.77	1.42	1.34	1.62	3.13	1.98	3.59
Total sugar and preserves		**4.99**	**5.76**	**5.44**	**6.14**	**7.64**	**9.22**	**11.77**	**10.18**	**14.08**
VEGETABLES:										
Potatoes		25.20	23.41	24.17	31.02	38.18	40.23	37.83	46.99	39.85
Fresh green		10.48	10.07	10.16	8.87	8.74	8.56	16.57	12.09	13.13
Other fresh		17.95	18.95	18.54	15.75	14.69	14.66	25.55	16.73	16.88
Frozen, including vegetable products		5.85	5.28	5.53	7.19	6.66	6.29	6.64	5.86	5.08
Other processed, including vegetable products		9.03	9.80	9.51	12.73	13.26	13.05	8.81	11.72	8.39
Total vegetables		**68.52**	**67.51**	**67.92**	**75.55**	**81.54**	**82.77**	**96.41**	**93.41**	**82.82**

Table 6 *continued*

	Income groups								
	Gross weekly income of head of household								
	Households with one or more earners						Households without an earner		OAP
	£645 and over	£475 and under £645	£475 and over	£250 and under £475	£125 and under £250	Less than £125	£125 or more	Less than £125	
	A1	A2	All A	B	C	D	E1	E2	
FRUIT:									
Fresh	25.30	26.82	26.27	21.47	18.25	14.88	38.20	20.78	23.86
Other, including fruit products	3.13	3.73	3.47	2.79	2.71	2.25	5.80	3.65	4.69
Fruit juices	14.47	11.73	12.80	8.64	5.35	3.47	9.46	4.08	2.44
Total fruit	**42.90**	**42.28**	**42.55**	**32.90**	**26.31**	**20.60**	**53.45**	**28.50**	**31.00**
CEREALS:									
Brown bread	3.46	3.58	3.52	3.25	3.28	2.78	5.58	3.60	4.87
White bread (standard loaves)	7.63	10.99	9.63	12.69	17.00	20.49	11.51	18.40	16.93
Wholewheat and wholemeal bread	3.77	3.18	3.42	3.76	3.38	2.18	6.35	4.59	5.39
Other bread	6.72	6.12	6.38	6.77	5.82	5.02	5.63	5.19	4.37
Total bread	21.57	23.86	22.96	26.47	29.49	30.48	29.07	31.78	31.57
Flour	2.43	2.59	2.51	2.58	2.96	4.49	5.69	3.94	5.44
Cakes	3.72	3.62	3.64	3.66	3.28	3.21	5.00	3.61	5.07
Biscuits	4.12	4.74	4.51	5.32	5.13	4.83	6.18	5.53	5.94
Oatmeal and oat products	0.70	0.55	0.62	0.44	0.40	0.46	1.01	0.64	1.02
Breakfast cereals	4.49	4.97	4.77	4.63	4.08	4.34	5.63	4.33	4.46
Other cereals	5.97	6.68	6.38	7.34	6.75	5.97	5.47	5.60	4.50
Total cereals	**43.00**	**47.01**	**45.41**	**50.43**	**52.11**	**53.79**	**58.04**	**55.41**	**58.00**
BEVERAGES:									
Tea	0.95	1.29	1.17	1.19	1.49	1.73	2.12	2.15	2.77
Coffee	0.93	0.64	0.74	0.63	0.55	0.58	1.10	0.59	0.63
Cocoa and drinking chocolate	0.24	0.17	0.21	0.16	0.13	0.24	0.20	0.19	0.09
Branded food drinks	0.05	0.05	0.05	0.11	0.15	0.08	0.25	0.30	0.41
Total beverages	**2.16**	**2.14**	**2.17**	**2.09**	**2.31**	**2.65**	**3.67**	**3.23**	**3.90**
MISCELLANEOUS:									
Soups, canned, dehydrated and powdered	2.13	2.04	2.07	2.33	2.55	2.64	3.04	2.85	3.38
Other foods	13.97	12.92	13.32	9.93	8.19	7.48	12.23	7.55	7.33
Total miscellaneous	**16.10**	**14.95**	**15.38**	**12.26**	**10.73**	**10.12**	**15.29**	**10.41**	**10.72**

Table 7
Household food expenditure by main food groups, according to income group for 1990

	Income groups								
	Gross weekly income of head of household								
	Households with one or more earners						Households without an earner		OAP
	£645 and over	£475 and under £645	£475 and over	£250 and under £475	£125 and under £250	Less than £125	£125 or more	Less than £125	
	A1	A2	All A	B	C	D	E1	E2	
MILK AND CREAM:									
Liquid wholemilk, full price	52.57	43.87	47.14	55.66	63.89	69.86	73.24	69.84	87.44
Welfare and school milk	0.23	0.16	0.19	0.15	0.12	0.10	...	0.05	...
Condensed milk	0.73	0.94	0.83	1.18	1.04	1.07	2.13	2.30	2.61
Dried and other milk	77.97	83.82	81.65	66.32	55.01	44.91	77.01	46.41	42.20
Cream	6.45	6.24	6.35	4.35	2.96	2.65	8.56	2.75	2.91
Total milk and cream	**137.94**	**135.04**	**136.16**	**127.64**	**123.01**	**118.59**	**160.95**	**121.34**	**135.16**
CHEESE:									
Natural	52.72	49.14	50.45	39.12	34.02	29.97	52.36	32.45	32.29
Processed	3.23	3.73	3.53	3.95	3.90	2.46	3.45	3.65	2.93
Total cheese	**55.95**	**52.87**	**53.97**	**43.08**	**37.92**	**32.43**	**55.81**	**36.10**	**35.22**
MEAT:									
Beef and veal	65.93	62.58	63.85	67.25	60.75	55.74	84.96	57.11	64.21
Mutton and lamb	35.54	33.02	34.19	25.51	26.41	27.61	47.31	32.21	35.71
Pork	36.55	23.23	28.65	29.93	29.82	26.69	33.03	26.31	26.55
Total carcase meat	138.03	118.83	126.69	122.69	116.99	110.05	165.31	115.62	126.47
Bacon and ham, uncooked	34.81	27.50	30.27	32.13	34.05	32.56	44.91	37.78	39.52
Poultry, uncooked	66.58	62.70	63.90	54.21	46.02	37.32	61.14	40.76	40.36
Other meat and meat products	135.37	131.34	133.30	135.10	138.56	119.38	123.57	117.65	111.66
Total meat	**374.79**	**340.39**	**354.15**	**344.13**	**335.61**	**299.33**	**394.94**	**311.81**	**318.02**
FISH:									
Fresh	22.49	15.95	18.69	13.13	10.63	10.35	48.86	17.43	21.55
Processed and shell	18.26	11.81	14.41	8.70	8.70	6.03	24.06	6.43	7.17
Prepared, including fish products	34.56	24.82	28.65	24.18	23.84	24.26	21.32	25.72	27.84
Frozen, including fish products	16.66	14.82	15.64	17.68	16.22	15.70	25.97	20.86	24.79
Total fish	**91.98**	**67.42**	**77.38**	**63.71**	**56.93**	**56.33**	**120.20**	**70.43**	**81.36**
EGGS	18.44	17.99	18.25	16.55	19.56	21.93	26.36	22.73	28.05
FATS:									
Butter	13.26	10.84	11.68	9.51	9.41	10.32	18.16	13.31	18.25
Margarine	7.69	8.70	8.32	8.91	9.87	9.98	11.22	12.79	14.49
Lard and compound cooking fat	0.93	1.25	1.12	1.41	1.90	2.17	1.89	2.62	3.21
Low-fat and dairy spreads	6.44	8.32	7.58	8.26	8.02	6.62	8.56	7.16	8.45
Other fats	7.31	5.66	6.37	5.75	5.24	3.23	5.69	4.93	5.55
Total fats	**35.64**	**34.77**	**35.07**	**33.84**	**34.44**	**32.32**	**45.51**	**40.82**	**49.96**
SUGAR AND PRESERVES:									
Sugar	5.96	7.83	7.09	8.85	11.39	13.39	16.33	14.86	19.27
Honey, preserves, syrup and treacle	8.03	7.52	7.66	6.05	5.29	6.54	13.77	8.02	14.22
Total sugar and preserves	**13.99**	**15.36**	**14.75**	**14.90**	**16.67**	**19.94**	**30.11**	**22.87**	**33.49**
VEGETABLES:									
Potatoes	26.91	23.99	25.12	25.89	27.69	29.24	30.88	32.60	28.68
Fresh green	33.06	28.12	29.77	21.47	18.13	16.99	35.71	23.66	23.70
Other fresh	61.47	61.56	61.50	48.92	40.29	39.93	60.43	41.13	38.75
Frozen, including vegetable products	20.68	18.24	19.27	23.97	20.66	17.25	20.73	17.24	15.23
Other processed, including vegetable products	48.63	40.21	51.87	59.01	55.36	49.62	33.00	45.45	29.30
Total vegetables	**190.76**	**185.68**	**187.53**	**179.25**	**162.11**	**153.01**	**180.75**	**160.09**	**135.66**

Table 7 *continued*

	Income groups								
	Gross weekly income of head of household								
	Households with one or more earners						Households without an earner		OAP
	£645 and over	£475 and under £645	£475 and over	£250 and under £475	£125 and under £250	Less than £125	£125 or more	Less than £125	
	A1	A2	All A	B	C	D	E1	E2	
FRUIT:									
Fresh	85.99	88.59	87.74	67.61	54.57	43.17	108.98	58.43	65.92
Other, including fruit products	20.39	22.63	21.73	13.77	11.65	9.64	27.88	15.36	19.54
Fruit juices	36.36	31.07	33.13	20.59	12.72	8.58	23.51	9.81	5.30
Total fruit	**142.73**	**142.28**	**142.60**	**101.97**	**78.94**	**61.39**	**160.38**	**83.59**	**90.76**
CEREALS:									
Brown bread	8.63	9.05	8.82	7.63	7.72	6.63	13.69	8.79	12.69
White bread (standard loaves)	15.82	22.42	19.76	24.37	31.90	37.34	23.82	35.14	35.27
Wholewheat and wholemeal bread	9.02	7.70	8.25	8.62	7.71	5.55	15.71	10.93	13.13
Other bread	27.38	23.68	25.22	26.12	21.55	18.21	23.22	18.45	16.96
Total bread	60.85	62.84	62.06	66.74	68.88	67.72	76.43	73.22	78.05
Flour	2.95	2.97	2.95	2.89	3.19	4.38	6.74	4.54	6.04
Cakes	31.72	32.72	32.16	29.20	25.74	24.10	38.67	27.68	38.40
Biscuits	28.87	32.01	30.90	33.13	30.91	26.92	35.97	30.31	31.23
Oatmeal and oat products	3.42	3.09	3.27	2.37	1.57	1.46	3.20	1.98	2.82
Breakfast cereals	28.12	30.35	29.40	27.48	24.34	25.64	30.88	25.20	25.75
Other cereals	48.07	52.07	50.60	49.63	41.85	35.36	32.18	28.88	20.15
Total cereals	**204.01**	**216.06**	**211.33**	**211.44**	**196.46**	**185.59**	**224.06**	**191.91**	**202.46**
BEVERAGES:									
Tea	13.74	17.56	16.25	16.13	19.62	21.99	26.85	27.43	36.26
Coffee	25.20	19.03	21.37	20.03	18.20	17.24	32.19	19.41	18.64
Cocoa and drinking chocolate	2.57	1.32	1.87	1.73	1.34	2.66	2.00	1.88	1.17
Branded food drinks	0.51	0.52	0.51	1.13	1.52	0.90	2.69	3.02	4.19
Total beverages	**42.01**	**38.43**	**40.01**	**39.02**	**40.68**	**42.79**	**63.72**	**51.74**	**60.26**
MISCELLANEOUS:									
Soups, canned, dehydrated and powdered	8.33	6.88	7.43	7.23	7.61	7.22	12.29	8.76	10.45
Other foods	57.47	54.72	55.80	47.19	40.02	35.71	52.10	37.33	32.48
Total miscellaneous	**65.83**	**61.61**	**63..25**	**54.40**	**47.62**	**42.93**	**64.40**	**46.08**	**42.92**
TOTAL EXPENDITURE	**£13.74**	**£13.08**	**£13.34**	**£12.30**	**£11.50**	**£10.67**	**£15.27**	**£11.60**	**£12.13**

Table 8

Household food expenditure by main food groups according to household composition for 1990

pence per person per week

	Households with											
No of adults	1		2					3	3 or more		4 or more	All households
No of children	0	1 or more	0	1	2	3	4 or more	0	1 or 2	3 or more	0	
MILK AND CREAM:												
Liquid wholemilk, full price	83.48	57.98	61.78	63.14	56.33	57.61	60.25	62.01	56.95	68.61	61.23	61.82
Welfare and school milk	–	0.41	–	0.13	0.33	0.32	–	–	0.03	–	–	0.12
Condensed milk	2.39	1.02	1.94	0.79	0.95	0.76	–	1.35	1.38	0.54	0.96	1.33
Dried and other milk	63.44	47.01	68.44	63.38	62.81	47.63	47.46	60.50	53.61	30.60	48.41	60.40
Cream	4.62	1.31	6.11	3.12	2.88	1.85	2.84	4.59	3.83	1.40	4.36	3.99
Total milk and cream	**153.94**	**107.75**	**138.26**	**135.56**	**123.31**	**108.17**	**110.56**	**128.44**	**115.80**	**101.14**	**114.95**	**127.66**
CHEESE:												
Natural	46.47	24.71	46.60	33.23	33.33	25.83	24.61	42.02	35.49	19.82	42.31	37.71
Processed	3.37	3.17	4.14	4.51	3.93	3.18	3.42	3.06	3.45	2.03	3.14	3.71
Total cheese	**49.84**	**27.88**	**50.73**	**37.73**	**37.26**	**29.01**	**28.04**	**45.08**	**38.94**	**21.85**	**45.45**	**41.42**
MEAT:												
Beef and veal	56.53	41.94	83.90	66.51	44.15	47.94	31.08	85.70	61.46	34.04	81.82	63.96
Mutton and lamb	33.43	15.97	40.94	27.89	18.62	12.47	21.65	37.43	24.32	24.12	30.07	28.60
Pork	26.98	19.40	35.39	30.55	22.59	21.77	24.61	36.55	30.11	18.93	33.12	29.12
Total carcase meat	116.93	77.31	160.23	124.96	85.36	82.18	77.33	159.68	115.88	77.09	145.01	121.68
Bacon and ham, uncooked	38.14	18.06	46.88	30.95	22.26	20.06	18.33	47.77	30.30	23.01	40.45	33.93
Poultry, uncooked	49.12	32.75	60.00	51.91	44.41	34.33	36.95	60.54	51.14	30.65	50.35	50.04
Other meat and meat products	158.37	108.26	149.02	147.57	110.09	93.14	78.88	144.82	130.23	75.98	155.88	131.64
Total meat	**362.53**	**236.38**	**416.11**	**355.39**	**262.12**	**229.71**	**211.49**	**412.81**	**327.55**	**206.74**	**391.69**	**337.32**
FISH:												
Fresh	22.98	4.66	26.80	11.49	7.90	4.17	2.92	16.91	11.68	5.51	14.11	15.06
Processed and shell	11.78	2.71	12.28	9.52	5.29	5.28	6.55	9.42	8.33	3.96	8.21	8.67
Prepared, including fish products	33.08	16.87	31.79	23.68	18.05	16.67	11.60	30.22	21.10	21.95	30.22	24.91
Frozen, including fish products	26.18	8.92	23.46	16.06	15.47	11.25	16.85	19.06	12.74	16.92	16.54	18.00
Total fish	**94.02**	**33.16**	**94.32**	**60.75**	**46.72**	**37.35**	**37.92**	**75.62**	**53.85**	**48.33**	**69.08**	**66.63**
EGGS	**28.57**	**15.30**	**24.72**	**17.78**	**14.55**	**14.63**	**14.84**	**21.98**	**16.12**	**14.55**	**17.21**	**19.51**
FATS:												
Butter	17.01	5.00	15.40	9.40	6.70	5.86	5.81	13.93	9.09	6.28	14.01	11.01
Margarine	12.95	9.78	11.87	8.88	8.51	8.47	7.30	10.26	8.36	7.19	10.40	9.97
Lard and compound cooking fat	1.98	1.12	2.53	1.20	1.06	1.84	1.76	2.36	1.52	0.82	2.25	1.80
Other fats	14.16	9.30	16.91	12.62	11.47	8.95	8.01	15.63	11.72	12.62	14.09	13.32
Total fats	**46.09**	**25.20**	**46.71**	**32.10**	**27.75**	**25.12**	**22.88**	**42.17**	**30.69**	**26.92**	**40.74**	**36.10**
SUGAR AND PRESERVES:												
Sugar	15.96	9.10	14.08	10.40	7.91	7.88	10.14	11.42	9.05	8.23	12.36	11.09
Honey, preserves, syrup and treacle	14.22	3.13	9.29	5.11	4.95	4.68	4.29	8.01	4.68	3.42	6.28	6.99
Total sugar and preserves	**30.18**	**12.22**	**23.37**	**15.51**	**12.86**	**12.57**	**14.44**	**19.42**	**13.74**	**11.66**	**18.65**	**18.06**
VEGETABLES:												
Potatoes	28.87	26.36	33.40	26.93	21.78	21.89	24.24	33.80	25.97	18.86	27.98	27.68
Fresh green	31.02	13.00	29.20	22.89	15.68	11.95	11.96	26.04	19.06	15.04	21.02	21.97
Other fresh	58.16	29.83	58.47	48.90	35.59	30.85	31.18	51.89	42.86	40.73	45.64	46.39
Frozen, including vegetable products	19.19	20.56	23.36	23.31	19.51	17.63	16.05	22.16	19.69	15.09	21.98	20.93
Other processed, incl vegetable products	51.46	50.26	51.52	60.51	55.01	49.99	50.79	50.92	50.43	44.41	55.60	52.81
Total vegetables	**188.69**	**140.01**	**195.93**	**182.53**	**147.55**	**132.31**	**134.21**	**184.80**	**158.02**	**134.13**	**172.23**	**169.76**

Table 8 *continued*

	Households with											
No of adults	1		2					3	3 or more		4 or more	All house holds
No of children	0	1 or more	0	1	2	3	4 or more	0	1 or 2	3 or more	0	
FRUIT:												
Fresh	94.30	39.70	82.85	61.84	54.09	42.57	50.78	70.15	50.97	37.02	63.16	65.07
Other, including fruit products	22.09	7.40	21.44	14.09	11.11	8.99	4.54	15.18	11.54	4.62	12.53	14.76
Fruit juices	17.33	10.68	19.25	20.86	19.73	12.91	10.75	13.33	15.02	14.54	17.34	17.25
Total fruit	**133.72**	**57.77**	**123.53**	**96.79**	**84.94**	**64.47**	**66.06**	**98.66**	**77.52**	**56.18**	**93.03**	**97.08**
CEREALS:												
Brown bread	13.70	5.18	11.24	7.31	6.00	5.27	2.67	9.69	7.09	3.25	7.28	8.32
White bread (standard loaves)	31.85	30.71	29.58	27.07	23.58	24.06	26.63	34.46	27.36	26.46	34.93	28.35
Wholewheat and wholemeal bread	16.79	5.54	12.60	7.39	6.04	5.93	5.86	9.44	5.41	3.07	8.48	8.97
Other bread	25.28	17.05	25.20	23.52	22.91	16.33	12.29	24.00	24.43	15.10	26.11	7.57
Total bread	87.62	58.49	78.62	65.27	58.53	51.58	47.46	77.59	64.29	47.88	76.81	68.60
Flour	4.47	1.94	4.82	1.89	2.48	2.40	8.37	3.36	2.85	8.23	3.23	3.54
Cakes	41.76	16.98	35.03	27.44	26.03	18.61	18.11	31.93	25.38	14.38	28.85	28.96
Biscuits	35.02	30.35	32.82	32.88	33.75	29.51	27.00	29.57	29.63	19.09	29.10	31.71
Oatmeal and oat products	3.40	1.19	2.83	2.28	2.16	1.55	1.44	1.41	1.36	2.06	2.45	2.22
Breakfast cereals	28.46	30.48	24.94	26.05	28.83	30.22	30.27	24.56	22.45	22.64	24.10	26.50
Other cereals	36.88	42.00	40.93	51.09	47.91	33.59	32.44	43.20	43.06	40.97	37.44	42.37
Total cereals	**237.61**	**181.45**	**219.99**	**206.90**	**199.70**	**167.46**	**165.10**	**211.63**	**189.02**	**155.24**	**201.98**	**203.88**
BEVERAGES:												
Tea	32.88	15.56	27.31	17.30	13.33	14.58	10.73	21.46	14.75	14.64	19.12	20.06
Coffee	27.24	14.82	25.34	17.97	14.55	14.63	11.38	22.95	15.51	12.22	25.42	19.85
Cocoa and drinking chocolate	1.72	1.96	1.57	1.84	1.82	1.34	3.27	1.87	1.20	1.23	1.50	1.68
Branded food drinks	3.73	0.51	2.94	0.94	0.61	0.37	–	1.36	1.02	–	1.64	1.58
Total beverages	**65.57**	**32.85**	**57.15**	**38.05**	**30.30**	**30.92**	**25.37**	**47.64**	**32.48**	**28.09**	**47.68**	**43.17**
MISCELLANEOUS:												
Soups, canned, dehydrated and powdered	12.35	6.52	9.54	7.94	6.05	6.65	3.66	6.99	6.58	8.66	7.97	7.89
Other foods	39.92	37.35	52.10	50.15	41.49	35.68	35.05	42.55	39.02	26.93	40.77	43.69
Total miscellaneous	**52.28**	**43.85**	**61.65**	**58.08**	**47.53**	**42.33**	**38.70**	**49.54**	**45.60**	**35.59**	**48.74**	**51.60**
TOTAL EXPENDITURE	**£14.43**	**£9.14**	**£14.52**	**£12.37**	**£10.35**	**£8.94**	**£8.70**	**£13.38**	**£10.99**	**£8.40**	**£12.61**	**£12.12**

Table 9

Household food consumption according to household composition groups within income groups: selected food items, annual averages, 1990

ounces per person per week [a]

Income group A

| | Adults only | Households [b] with | | | | 3 or more adults, 1 or more children |
| | | 2 adults and | | | | |
		1 child	2 children	3 children	4 or more children [c]	
Miilk and cream (pt or eq pt)	3.63	4.23	3.80	3.33	2.85	3.54
Cheese	6.32	3.83	4.16	3.97	5.65	4.21
Carcase meat	13.87	11.00	8.13	6.99	6.95	8.90
Other meat and meat products	28.32	19.98	16.28	14.75	11.86	20.87
Fish	6.18	5.29	3.95	4.01	5.73	4.43
Eggs (no)	2.51	2.36	1.41	1.44	2.70	1.52
Fats	9.37	7.15	6.00	7.81	11.24	6.32
Sugar and preserves	6.62	6.77	4.47	6.24	6.81	3.51
Potatoes	29.29	23.58	19.60	23.21	15.62	23.93
Fresh green vegetables	13.66	10.86	7.40	7.81	4.49	9.71
Other fresh vegetables	24.73	21.58	13.84	15.46	19.35	13.92
Processed vegetables	17.14	18.68	13.32	14.99	13.86	11.34
Fresh fruit	33.71	26.37	21.11	24.41	27.73	21.26
Other fruit and fruit products	19.14	19.16	16.14	15.22	27.54	12.15
Bread	27.08	22.88	20.52	17.83	24.73	22.03
Other cereals	23.31	22.30	23.19	23.28	34.05	19.06
Tea	1.89	1.19	0.63	1.05	0.35	0.79
Coffee	1.08	0.95	0.55	0.72	0.54	0.34
Cocoa and drinking chocolate	0.19	0.17	0.37	0.15	–	0.06
Branded food drinks	0.05	–	0.07	–	–	0.07
TOTAL EXPENDITURE	£16.82	£14.87	£11.58	£10.18	£11.54	£11.56

Income group B

| | Adults only | 1 adult, 1 or more children | Households with | | | | 3 or more adults, 1 or more children |
| | | | 2 adults and | | | | |
			1 child	2 children	3 children	4 or more children	
Milk and cream (pt or eq pt)	3.85	3.69	3.82	3.57	3.47	3.48	3.62
Cheese	4.92	5.45	3.83	3.80	3.15	3.82	3.95
Carcase meat	13.62	4.02	11.42	8.22	10.79	16.89	10.57
Other meat and meat products	27.21	18.83	23.35	20.21	17.58	19.54	22.13
Fish	6.49	3.29	4.39	3.71	3.14	4.02	4.36
Eggs	2.15	0.93	1.76	1.61	1.43	1.97	1.94
Fats	9.91	5.88	7.78	7.40	5.83	10.22	8.82
Sugar and preserves	7.11	3.03	6.07	5.54	4.75	6.79	5.88
Potatoes	35.03	17.10	31.33	25.37	27.64	34.16	33.82
Fresh green vegetables	12.00	6.45	8.43	6.50	5.55	6.72	8.49
Other fresh vegetables	19.85	8.24	16.12	12.46	10.36	10.97	16.15
Processed vegetables	21.61	16.59	20.09	18.64	17.11	21.67	19.69
Fresh fruit	27.36	20.59	20.04	18.38	15.34	17.96	18.21
Other fruit and fruit products	12.87	19.03	11.08	11.95	8.01	4.45	10.04
Bread	29.36	27.17	25.77	24.82	22.97	23.42	25.72
Other cereals	24.29	30.62	23.21	23.93	22.06	26.19	24.55
Tea	1.42	0.90	1.18	1.02	1.16	0.74	1.02
Coffee	0.85	0.53	0.54	0.50	0.38	0.83	0.54
Cocoa and drinking chocolate	0.13	–	0.24	0.16	0.13	0.67	0.12
Branded food drinks	0.20	–	0.07	0.06	0.02	0.00	0.14
TOTAL EXPENDITURE	£14.64	£12.12	£12.40	£10.80	£9.17	£9.99	£11.43

Table 9 *continued*

ounces per person per week [a]

	Income group C						
		Households with					
	Adults only	1 adult, 1 or more children	2 adults and				3 or more adults, 1 or more children
			1 child	2 children	3 children	4 or more children	
Milk and cream (pt or eq pt)	3.94	3.71	3.99	3.62	3.46	3.41	3.11
Cheese	4.49	3.23	3.53	3.36	2.26	2.32	3.04
Carcase meat	13.69	9.70	9.93	7.43	7.55	6.18	10.38
Other meat and meat products	26.56	22.35	25.29	19.96	17.85	19.47	21.19
Fish	5.80	1.97	4.09	3.49	3.11	2.88	3.54
Eggs (no)	2.71	1.41	2.10	1.70	2.27	1.34	1.94
Fats	10.69	7.11	8.41	6.68	6.94	6.24	6.92
Sugar and preserves	8.83	5.22	7.45	5.92	6.42	6.93	7.16
Potatoes	43.58	20.83	33.68	30.13	36.40	46.40	35.68
Fresh green vegetables	11.22	4.25	8.86	5.79	5.84	4.85	6.80
Other fresh vegetables	17.81	13.41	14.81	10.98	10.85	7.99	12.50
Processed vegetables	20.95	21.78	21.57	19.22	19.00	16.70	17.01
Fresh fruit	22.68	16.72	16.50	14.14	12.27	19.58	12.36
Other fruit and fruit products	9.37	8.66	10.14	6.41	5.20	2.63	6.43
Bread	32.78	19.56	30.19	26.36	24.07	25.40	27.23
Other cereals	24.06	23.74	21.20	23.12	20.10	23.23	19.12
Tea	1.81	1.19	1.42	1.16	0.94	0.99	1.28
Coffee	0.69	0.63	0.52	0.37	0.50	0.18	0.45
Cocoa and drinking chocolate	0.15	0.11	0.10	0.09	0.06	0.16	0.15
Branded food drinks	0.27	0.16	0.08	0.05	0.01	–	0.03
TOTAL EXPENDITURE	£13.54	£10.51	£11.75	£9.34	£8.54	£8.46	£9.36

	Income group D and E2						
		Households with					
	Adults only	1 adult, 1 or more children	2 adults and				3 or more adults, 1 or more children
			1 child	2 children	3 children	4 or more children [c]	
Milk and cream (pt or eq pt)	4.33	3.85	3.94	3.03	3.07	3.58	3.30
Cheese	4.38	2.53	3.02	2.57	2.19	1.54	2.51
Carcase meat	13.05	6.99	12.36	8.92	7.52	6.48	10.66
Other meat and meat products	26.40	18.59	25.64	19.88	18.77	15.15	19.88
Fish	7.16	2.72	6.16	3.31	1.71	2.26	4.89
Eggs (no)	3.14	2.01	2.79	1.78	2.21	2.16	2.20
Fats	12.89	7.05	7.37	6.44	7.39	4.10	9.49
Sugar and preserves	12.67	0.31	7.92	5.16	6.65	6.88	7.86
Potatoes	50.55	39.19	45.92	34.28	43.38	26.82	35.39
Fresh green vegetables	15.08	5.84	8.01	5.68	4.35	2.74	9.48
Other fresh vegetables	20.74	8.58	13.33	12.53	7.03	8.76	16.66
Processed vegetables	18.34	17.97	20.82	19.59	18.90	15.27	15.72
Fresh fruit	25.60	10.40	16.65	11.64	6.21	11.44	10.42
Other fruit and fruit products	9.98	3.85	5.76	4.34	2.23	1.59	1.99
Bread	35.40	27.83	30.51	24.22	30.34	18.18	26.40
Other cereals	26.60	19.24	20.60	17.77	14.84	32.29	17.81
Tea	2.67	1.17	1.74	0.87	1.35	1.06	1.39
Coffee	0.77	0.32	0.75	0.54	0.30	0.19	0.41
Cocoa and drinking chocolate	0.20	0.27	0.15	0.27	0.24	0.34	0.00
Branded food drinks	0.37	0.02	0.25	0.00	0.18	0.00	0.04
TOTAL EXPENDITURE	£13.81	£8.30	£11.02	£8.12	£7.30	£6.69	£8.83

(a) Except where otherwise stated.

(b) Averages are not shown for households of 1 adult and 1 or more children or 2 adults with 4 or more children in income group A because there are fewer than 10 such households in the sample.

(c) The figures in this column are based on a sample of more than 9 but fewer than 20 households.

Table 10

Nutritional value of household food: national averages, 1988-1990

		1988	1989	1990
		(i) Consumption per person per day		
Energy	(kcal)	1,998	1,941	1,872
	(MJ)	8.4	8.1	7.9
Total protein	(g)	67.8	65.9	63.1
Animal protein	(g)	41.9	40.8	38.7
Fat	(g)	93	90	86
Fatty acids:				
saturated	(g)	38.3	36.9	34.6
monounsaturated	(g)	33.8	33.1	31.8
polyunsaturated	(g)	14.2	13.6	13.9
Carbohydrate[a]	(g)	237	230	224
Calcium	(mg)	860	840	820
Iron	(mg)	10.9	10.6	10.4
Thiamin	(mg)	1.39	1.32	1.28
Riboflavin	(mg)	1.68	1.64	1.61
Niacin	(mg)	12.9	12.3	11.7
Niacin equivalent	(mg)	27.4	26.4	25.1
Vitamin C	(mg)	61	54	52
Vitamin A:				
retinol	(µg)	880	820	780
β-carotene	(µg)	2,370	2,440	1,880
total (retinol equivalent)	(µg)	1,270	1,220	1,100
Vitamin D[c]	(µg)	3.09	3.04	3.02
		(ii) As a percentage of recommended intake[b]		
Energy		91	88	86
Protein		123	120	115
(as a percentage of minimum requirement)		167	163	157
Calcium		159	156	153
Iron		102	100	99
Thiamin		153	146	142
Riboflavin		123	121	119
Niacin equivalent		177	171	164
Vitamin C		213	190	185
Vitamin A (retinol equivalent)		184	177	160

(a) available carbohydrate, calculated as monosaccharide

(b) estimates of percentage adequacy are based on the recommendations of the Department of Health and Social Security (1979). In deriving these percentages, a conventional deduction of 10 per cent is made from the consumption figures given in Section (i) of the table to allow for wastage.

(c) contributions from pharmaceutical sources of this (or any other) vitamin are not recorded by the Survey.

Table 11

Nutritional value of household food in different regions, 1990

		Region									
		Scotland	Wales	England	North	Yorkshire and Humber side	North West	East Midlands	West Midlands	South West	South East/ East Anglia
(i) Consumption per person per day											
Energy	(kcal)	1,980	1,929	1,857	1,971	1,898	1,727	1,883	1,868	1,988	1,830
	(MJ)	8.3	8.1	7.8	8.3	8.0	7.3	7.9	7.8	8.3	7.7
Total protein	(g)	65.8	64.2	62.7	66.0	65.0	59.5	64.1	62.9	65.3	61.6
Animal protein	(g)	39.4	39.1	38.5	39.3	40.0	37.0	39.6	38.0	39.9	38.2
Fat	(g)	89	90	86	88	87	79	88	86	93	86
Fatty acids:											
saturated	(g)	36.0	36.1	34.3	35.5	34.6	32.1	34.7	34.0	37.4	34.1
monounsaturated	(g)	32.6	33.3	31.6	32.6	32.4	28.9	32.8	31.9	34.1	31.3
polyunsaturated	(g)	14.1	14.5	13.8	13.7	13.9	12.1	14.6	13.7	15.1	13.9
Carbohydrate	(g)	244	229	222	243	227	208	221	225	236	217
Calcium	(mg)	840	803	816	837	852	757	861	782	870	812
Iron	(mg)	11.1	10.3	10.3	11.2	10.5	9.6	10.4	10.1	10.8	10.2
Thiamin	(mg)	1.33	1.31	1.27	1.36	1.30	1.20	1.30	1.30	1.30	1.20
Riboflavin	(mg)	1.65	1.59	1.60	1.63	1.65	1.53	1.66	1.54	1.69	1.60
Niacin	(mg)	11.8	11.7	11.7	12.1	11.9	10.9	11.8	11.7	12.2	11.8
Niacin equivalent	(mg)	25.8	25.3	25.0	26.1	25.7	23.5	25.4	24.9	26.1	24.9
Vitamin C	(mg)	50	47	53	53	52	45	52	47	57	57S
Vitamin A:											
retinol	(µg)	835	768	779	839	853	751	740	691	884	767
β-carotene	(µg)	1,770	2,006	1,877	1,873	1,916	1,782	1,991	1,807	1,910	1,898
total (retinol equivalent)	(µg)	1,130	1,103	1,092	1,151	1,173	1,048	1,072	992	1,202	1,083
Vitamin D	(µg)	2.95	3.25	3.02	3.28	3.17	2.78	2.90	3.11	3.28	2.94
(ii) As a percentage of recommended intake[a]											
Energy		89	88	85	90	87	81	83	83	89	85
Protein		118	117	115	121	119	111	113	111	117	115
(as a percentage of minimum requirement)		161	158	156	165	162	151	154	152	159	156
Calcium		155	152	153	158	159	144	156	142	160	155
Iron		104	98	98	107	100	93	96	94	101	99
Thiamin		145	146	141	151	145	136	139	138	146	140
Riboflavin		120	116	119	122	123	116	119	112	123	121
Niacin equivalent		165	163	164	171	168	157	161	159	167	165
Vitamin C		173	164	188	188	184	164	179	161	195	205
Vitamin A (retinol equivalent)		162	159	160	169	172	157	152	142	171	161

(a) estimates of percentage adequacy are based on the recommendations of the Department of Health and Social Security (1979).

Table 12

Nutritional value of household food in different income groups, 1990

		Income groups						
		Gross weekly income of head of household						OAP
		Households with one or more earners				Household without an earner		
		£475 and over	£250 and under £475	£125 and under £250	Less than £125	£125 or more	Less than £125	
		A	B	C	D	E1	E2	
		(i) Consumption per person per day						
Energy	(kcal)	1,698	1,810	1,851	1,892	2,217	2,032	2,147
	(MJ)	7.1	7.6	7.8	7.9	9.3	8.5	9.0
Total protein	(g)	58.8	61.9	62.5	62.7	76.0	66.2	68.2
Animal protein	(g)	37.0	38.1	38.0	37.8	47.5	39.7	41.9
Fat	(g)	79	84	85	86	99	93	99
Fatty acids:								
saturated	(g)	32.1	33.4	33.8	34.7	41.0	37.3	40.4
monounsaturated	(g)	28.8	31.1	31.5	31.6	36.0	34.4	36.1
polyunsaturated	(g)	12.8	13.8	13.6	13.2	15.0	14.9	15.2
Carbohydrate	(g)	199	214	223	232	272	247	262
Calcium	(mg)	799	798	798	816	1008	849	901
Iron	(mg)	9.9	10.3	10.2	10.2	12.5	10.9	11.2
Thiamin	(mg)	1.19	1.24	1.26	1.27	1.57	1.38	1.41
Riboflavin	(mg)	1.55	1.57	1.56	1.57	2.00	1.69	1.84
Niacin	(mg)	11.5	11.7	11.4	11.2	14.6	12.0	12.1
Niacin equivalent	(mg)	24.0	24.8	24.7	24.5	30.7	26.1	26.6
Vitamin C	(mg)	62	53	48	44	72	51	48
Vitamin A:								
retinol	(µg)	725	739	755	761	889	859	1,109
β-carotene	(µg)	1,975	1,868	1,785	1,620	2,737	1,849	1,947
total (retinol equivalent)	(µg)	1,054	1,050	1,052	1,031	1,346	1,168	1,434
Vitamin D	(µg)	2.76	2.83	2.87	2.90	4.01	3.58	4.82
		(ii) As a percentage of recommended intake[a]						
Energy		82	83	83	86	101	93	100
Protein		113	114	111	113	137	121	126
(as a percentage of minimum requirement)		155	157	155	154	172	159	155
Calcium		154	151	151	146	188	152	167
Iron		97	98	96	94	116	100	103
Thiamin		139	139	137	139	171	153	157
Riboflavin		122	120	116	115	133	121	122
Niacin equivalent		166	167	161	158	180	163	154
Vitamin C		235	195	170	151	230	171	148
Vitamin A (retinol equivalent)		165	159	154	149	173	161	179

(a) estimates of percentage adequacy are based on the recommendations of the Department of Health and Social Security (1979).

Table 13
Nutritional value of food in households of different composition, 1990

		Households with										
No of adults		1		2					3	3 or more		4 or more
No of children		0	1 or more	0	1	2	3	4 or more	0	1 or 2	3 or more	0
(i) *Consumption per person per day*												
Energy	(kcal)	2,168	1,611	2,169	1,813	1,611	1,526	1,674	2,017	1,721	1,515	2,003
	(MJ)	9.1	6.8	9.1	7.6	6.8	6.4	7.0	8.5	7.2	6.3	8.4
Total protein	(g)	71.7	52.9	73.5	61.8	53.9	51.2	54.2	70.7	58.4	48.1	66.1
Animal protein	(g)	43.7	31.1	45.9	38.3	32.4	30.6	30.9	44.2	35.9	28.3	40.4
Fat	(g)	98	72	102	84	73	68	72	95	80	70	97
Fatty acids:												
saturated	(g)	40.6	28.4	40.7	33.5	29.2	27.3	28.5	38.3	31.7	25.4	37.4
monounsaturated	(g)	35.6	26.6	37.7	30.9	26.5	25.2	26.4	34.9	29.7	26.4	35.8
polyunsaturated	(g)	14.9	12.0	16.3	13.6	11.6	10.9	11.7	14.4	13.1	13.6	16.5
Carbohydrate	(g)	266	200	255	216	198	188	216	235	204	184	232
Calcium	(mg)	966	731	918	805	740	680	742	859	750	653	823
Iron	(mg)	12.0	9.0	11.8	10.4	9.1	9.0	9.2	11.1	9.3	7.8	10.7
Thiamin	(mg)	1.47	1.10	1.47	1.24	1.11	1.08	1.15	1.39	1.16	1.00	1.32
Riboflavin	(mg)	1.92	1.43	1.84	1.60	1.41	1.39	1.37	1.70	1.43	1.22	1.63
Niacin	(mg)	13.0	9.5	13.9	11.7	9.9	9.8	9.7	13.2	10.7	8.6	12.6
Niacin equivalent	(mg)	28.2	20.8	29.4	24.8	21.4	20.6	21.2	28.1	23.1	18.9	26.5
Vitamin C	(mg)	60	39	62	55	46	42	40	54	47	41	53
Vitamin A:												
retinol	(µg)	994	610	969	779	606	582	550	854	653	583	962
β-carotene	(µg)	2,108	1,256	2,275	2,036	1,585	1,461	1,204	2,046	1,765	1,389	1,874
total (retinol equivalent)	(µg)	1,345	819	1,348	1,118	870	826	751	1,196	947	815	1,275
Vitamin D	(µg)	3.89	2.41	3.70	2.95	2.54	2.48	2.52	3.09	2.50	2.12	2.92
(ii) *As a percentage of recommended intake*[a]												
Energy		101	85	95	85	76	74	81	87	77	71	88
Protein		133	110	128	115	102	99	104	122	104	89	116
(as a percentage of minimum requirement)		170	159	168	160	144	141	150	164	143	125	157
Calcium		188	131	178	149	132	118	125	172	143	118	170
Iron		114	88	110	100	88	87	88	105	88	75	104
Thiamin		165	140	155	141	128	128	136	146	126	115	140
Riboflavin		134	129	125	124	114	115	114	118	104	95	116
Niacin equivalent		172	163	176	169	151	151	155	171	148	129	166
Vitamin C		195	157	202	199	177	165	159	180	169	157	182
Vitamin A (retinol equivalent)		176	146	177	171	142	141	130	161	137	129	177

(a) estimates of percentage adequacy are based on the recommendations of the Department of Health and Social Security (1979).

Table 14

Contributions made by selected foods to the nutritional value of household food: national averages, 1990

per person per day

| | Energy | Fat | Fatty Acids | | Sugars[a] | Starch[b] | Fibre[c] |
			Saturated	Poly-unsaturated			
	kcal	g	g	g	g	g	g
Milk and milk products	253	14.5	9.1	0.5	17.2	0.1	...
of which: liquid milk	121	7.1	4.5	0.2	8.7	–	–
yoghurt	11	0.1	0.1	...	2.1	0.1	–
cheese	61	5.0	3.2	0.2	0.1	–	–
Meat and meat products	293	22.4	8.7	2.2	0.4	4.5	0.2
of which: carcase meat	106	8.7	3.5	0.7	–	–	–
poultry, uncooked	33	2.1	0.7	0.4	–	–	–
offal	3	0.1	...	...	...	–	–
other meat and meat products	152	11.5	4.5	1.1	0.3	2.6	0.1
Fish	30	1.6	0.4	0.5	0.1	0.7	...
Eggs	24	1.7	0.5	0.2	–	–	–
Fats	261	28.7	10.0	6.5	0.4	0.1	–
of which: butter	48	5.3	3.6	0.2	–	–	–
margarine	94	10.4	3.0	2.9	0.1	–	–
low fat and dairy spreads	32	3.4	1.1	0.7	0.1	–	–
vegetable and salad oils	51	5.7	0.6	2.3	–	–	–
Sugar and preserves	115	...	...	...	30.4	0.1	...
Vegetables	185	3.2	0.8	1.1	6.7	28.2	4.8
of which: potatoes	82	0.1	...	0.1	1.3	17.9	1.3
other fresh vegetables	12	0.1	...	0.1	1.8	0.3	0.9
frozen vegetables	21	0.6	0.1	0.2	0.6	2.8	0.8
canned vegetables	21	0.2	...	0.1	1.3	2.4	0.9
Fruit	71	1.3	0.3	0.4	14.2	0.4	1.3
of which: fresh fruit	33	0.2	...	...	7.5	0.3	1.0
fruit juices	13	–	–	–	3.5	–	...
Cereals	590	11.1	4.2	1.9	17.3	96.2	5.5
of which: white bread	135	0.9	0.2	0.3	1.7	26.9	0.9
brown and wholemeal bread	64	0.7	0.1	0.2	0.6	11.9	1.4
cakes, pastries and biscuits	153	6.6	3.1	0.7	9.2	13.1	0.6
breakfast cereals	63	0.4	0.1	0.2	2.6	11.3	1.2
Other foods	50	1.9	0.6	0.6	5.6	1.6	0.2
Total all foods	**1,872**	**86.4**	**34.6**	**13.9**	**92.3**	**131.7**	**12.1**

Table 14 *continued*

	Calcium	Iron	Sodium	Vitamin C	Vitamin A[d]	Vitamin D
	mg	mg	mg	mg	µg	µg
Milk and milk products	473	0.3	288	2.7	190	0.26
of which: liquid milk	207	0.1	99	1.2	99	0.26
yoghurt	23	...	10	0.1	1	...
cheese	102	...	112	–	54	0.04
Meat and meat products	21	1.8	491	1.0	352	0.02
of which: carcase meat	3	0.6	24	–	1	–
poultry, uncooked	1	0.1	12	–	6	–
offal	...	0.2	2	0.3	292	0.01
other meat and meat products	17	0.3	452	0.7	54	...
Fish	16	0.2	54	...	1	0.56
Eggs	9	0.3	22	–	31	0.28
Fats	4	...	183	...	231	1.52
of which: butter	1	...	49	–	58	0.05
margarine	2	...	95	–	113	1.03
low fat and dairy spreads	1	...	40	–	61	0.46
vegetable and salad oils	–	–	–	–	–	–
Sugar and preserves	3	...	3	0.5	...	...
Vegetables	50	2.0	233	22.9	262	...
of which: potatoes	5	0.4	11	7.7	–	–
other fresh vegetables	17	0.3	9	6.1	199	–
frozen vegetables	6	0.2	9	3.6	31	–
canned vegetables	11	0.4	122	0.8	14	–
Fruit	17	0.3	12	23.7	6	...
of which: fresh fruit	10	0.1	3	12.3	5	–
fruit juices	3	0.1	3	10.7	–	–
Cereals	201	5.1	958	0.8	12	0.37
of which: white bread	61	0.9	314	–	–	–
brown and wholemeal bread	23	0.8	163	–	–	–
cakes, pastries and biscuits	33	0.7	124	...	5	0.04
breakfast cereals	8	1.6	134	0.5	–	0.29
Other foods	22	0.5	257	0.7	11	0.02
Total all foods	**817**	**10.4**	**2,501**	**52.3**	**1,096**	**3.02**

(a) Includes sucrose, glucose, fructose, lactose and other simple sugars, as their monosaccharide equivalents

(b) As its monosaccharide equivalent

(c) As non-starch polysaccharides

(d) Retinol equivalent

Appendix C

Tables of Historical Data

List of tables

		page
1.	Household consumption and expenditure for main food groups, 1950 to 1990	93
2.	Consumption of selected foods, 1942 to 1990	94
3.	Household food consumption by main food groups, according to region, for 1955 to 1990	99
4.	Household food consumption by main food groups, according to income group, for 1952 to 1990	102
5.	Household food expenditure by main food groups, according to income group, for 1952 to 1990	105
6.	Household food consumption by main food groups, according to household composition, 1952 to 1990	108
7.	Household food expenditure by main food groups, according to household composition, 1952 to 1990	111
8.	Nutritional value of household food : national averages, 1940 to 1990	114

Table 1

Household consumption and expenditure for main food groups, 1950 to 1990

Consumption

ounces per person per week, except where otherwise stated

	1950	1955	1960	1965	1970	1975	1980	1985	1990
Milk and cream (pt or eq pt)	5.21	5.09	5.14	5.19	5.08	5.12	4.58	4.13	3.82
Cheese	2.54	2.83	3.04	3.20	3.59	3.79	3.89	3.91	4.00
Meat	29.85	34.42	35.89	37.60	39.53	37.12	40.19	36.77	34.11
Fish	6.62	5.95	5.86	5.78	5.35	4.46	4.80	4.90	5.08
Eggs (no)	3.50	4.19	4.64	4.78	4.66	4.14	3.69	3.15	2.20
Fats	11.61	11.88	11.97	11.86	11.95	11.14	11.22	10.07	9.00
Sugar and preserves	16.43	21.73	20.97	20.55	19.51	13.72	13.22	10.27	7.73
Vegetables	98.68	97.06	95.44	92.62	92.37	83.98	85.37	84.92	79.79
Fruit	18.09	21.91	24.62	25.56	25.52	23.94	28.06	27.06	31.56
Cereals	81.67	80.04	70.56	65.79	63.19	57.18	55.41	53.84	51.79
Beverages	2.72	3.54	3.57	3.44	3.61	3.11	3.00	2.70	2.47

Expenditure

pence per person per week

	1950	1955	1960	1965	1970	1975	1980	1985	1990
Milk and cream	8.91	12.83	15.38	18.19	22.34	35.75	80.24	98.66	127.69
Cheese	1.10	2.45	3.27	3.79	4.68	10.38	23.83	31.32	41.43
Meat	17.25	35.30	42.11	50.70	64.61	117.95	230.48	273.51	337.24
Fish	3.43	4.71	6.53	7.73	8.93	15.72	32.12	44.54	66.62
Eggs	3.94	7.23	7.69	7.45	8.15	12.54	19.22	21.10	19.49
Fats	4.24	9.46	9.44	10.45	10.65	18.13	33.15	36.77	36.11
Sugar and preserves	3.24	5.35	5.28	5.89	5.74	12.94	16.38	17.36	18.08
Vegetables	9.50	13.72	15.58	18.53	25.11	49.14	80.22	113.04	169.45
Fruit	4.15	7.88	9.03	10.76	12.22	22.84	43.91	60.39	97.13
Cereals	13.89	19.17	22.70	26.18	32.20	57.37	109.85	144.12	203.98
Beverages	2.82	7.53	7.54	7.50	8.88	11.57	27.69	41.57	43.18
Miscellaneous	1.53	2.69	3.67	5.06	7.20	13.05	24.42	35.02	51.67
TOTAL EXPENDITURE	£0.74	£1.28	£1.48	£1.72	£2.11	£3.77	£7.21	£9.17	£12.12

Table 2
Consumption of selected foods, 1942 to 1990

MILK, CHEESE AND EGGS

ounces per person per week [a]

	Liquid [b] wholemilk	Skimmed milk	Yoghurt	Total milk and cream	Natural cheese	Processed cheese	Total cheese	Eggs
1942	3.48			3.76			3.58	1.40
1943	3.94			4.30			3.07	2.22
1944	3.97			4.41			2.61	2.93
1945	4.11			4.43			2.49	3.01
1946	3.95			4.31			2.54	2.50
1947	3.85			4.30			2.20	2.13
1948	4.02			4.34			2.00	2.23
1949	4.36			4.71			2.15	2.97
1950	4.78			5.17			2.54	3.50
1951	4.90			5.21			2.76	2.84
1952	4.82			5.09			2.17	2.98
1953	4.78			5.07			2.50	3.99
1954	4.81			5.08			2.90	4.26
1955	4.81			5.09	2.46	0.37	2.83	4.19
1956	4.83			5.11	2.45	0.40	2.85	4.35
1957	4.84			5.10	2.52	0.37	2.89	4.41
1958	4.80			5.10	2.60	0.38	2.98	4.42
1959	4.76			5.07	2.52	0.40	2.92	4.54
1960	4.84			5.14	2.64	0.40	3.04	4.64
1961	4.90			5.20	2.70	0.37	3.07	4.66
1962	4.95			5.26	2.76	0.36	3.12	4.68
1963	4.98			5.31	2.81	0.35	3.16	4.58
1964	4.85			5.16	2.77	0.40	3.17	4.73
1965	4.85			5.19	2.84	0.36	3.20	4.78
1966	4.93			5.31	2.77	0.34	3.11	4.77
1967	4.89			5.27	3.00	0.35	3.35	4.72
1968	4.82			5.22	3.08	0.33	3.41	4.66
1969	4.89			5.29	3.15	0.35	3.50	4.60
1970	4.63			5.08	3.25	0.34	3.59	4.66
1971	4.74			5.16	3.25	0.38	3.63	4.55
1972	4.62	0.01	0.04	5.05	3.23	0.30	3.53	4.41
1973	4.75	0.01	0.04	5.17	3.41	0.34	3.75	4.23
1974	4.74	0.01	0.05	5.13	3.47	0.27	3.74	4.09
1975	4.76	0.01	0.04	5.12	3.51	0.28	3.79	4.14
1976	4.71	0.01	0.05	5.08	3.50	0.29	3.79	4.08
1977	4.54	0.02	0.05	4.90	3.56	0.24	3.80	4.00
1978	4.44	0.02	0.06	4.82	3.49	0.23	3.72	3.96
1979	4.31	0.03	0.07	4.74	3.61	0.23	3.84	3.88
1980	4.16	0.04	0.08	4.58	3.66	0.23	3.89	3.69
1981	4.01	0.07	0.09	4.46	3.65	0.24	3.89	3.68
1982	3.95	0.08	0.09	4.40	3.55	0.25	3.80	3.51
1983	3.80	0.12	0.10	4.30	3.77	0.24	4.01	3.53
1984	3.61	0.33	0.11	4.31	3.60	0.24	3.84	3.21
1985	3.32	0.43	0.13	4.13	3.65	0.26	3.91	3.15
1986	3.04	0.70	0.14	4.15	3.90	0.26	4.16	3.01
1987	2.88	0.78	0.14	4.07	3.80	0.29	4.09	2.89
1988	2.65	0.93	0.16	4.00	3.84	0.29	4.13	2.67
1989	2.42	1.09	0.16	3.93	3.76	0.31	4.07	2.29
1990	2.17	1.25	0.17	3.82	3.70	0.30	4.00	2.20

(a) Except milks and yoghurt (pints), eggs (number), and fruit juices (fluid ounces).
(b) Including welfare and school milk.

Table 2 *continued*

FRUIT AND VEGETABLES

	Oranges and other citrus	Apples and pears	Bananas	Total fresh fruit	Fruit juice	Total other fruit [c]	Potatoes	Fresh green vegetables	Other fresh vegetables	Other vegetables and products
1942				6.94			66.20	15.45	15.88	4.81
1943				7.89			68.59	19.08	15.46	5.33
1944	1.19			9.23			68.98	20.01	16.84	5.26
1945	2.64			11.20			65.73	18.52	15.58	6.62
1946	2.28			10.67			70.52	17.64	15.74	7.37
1947	4.54			15.29			67.21	12.65	18.52	8.43
1948	3.65			14.45			59.59	17.41	17.08	7.73
1949	3.13			13.64			65.39	14.86	17.29	8.18
1950	3.27	7.09	1.29	14.41	0.25	3.68	62.04	13.81	15.28	7.55
1951	4.57	8.09	1.57	17.80	0.27	3.93	62.21	15.56	16.69	7.97
1952	3.41	7.88	1.44	16.34	0.22	3.37	64.07	16.31	15.83	8.05
1953	4.31	7.02	2.55	17.02	0.23	4.09	62.77	16.54	15.87	7.08
1954	3.80	6.35	2.91	15.99	0.25	4.95	62.12	14.79	13.98	7.32
1955	3.82	6.70	2.93	16.11	0.29	5.80	59.90	14.63	14.64	7.89
1956	3.72	6.58	3.40	16.42	0.37	5.66	57.30	14.14	14.36	8.85
1957	3.85	7.29	3.40	16.63	0.40	6.13	57.38	15.73	14.55	8.09
1958	3.42	6.36	3.08	15.26	0.37	5.78	54.15	14.39	14.27	9.32
1959	4.03	8.17	3.37	18.54	0.44	6.14	53.99	14.70	14.31	9.05
1960	4.36	8.12	3.39	18.41	0.48	6.21	56.03	15.18	15.05	9.18
1961	3.98	7.10	3.56	17.32	0.50	6.37	56.69	14.44	14.22	9.93
1962	4.20	7.15	3.64	17.87	0.48	6.55	52.36	14.37	13.84	9.69
1963	3.80	7.79	3.31	17.91	0.52	6.69	55.57	12.48	14.11	10.60
1964	4.37	7.95	3.31	18.35	0.58	6.79	54.11	13.86	14.67	10.59
1965	4.32	8.14	3.56	18.79	0.67	6.77	53.24	14.34	14.33	10.71
1966	4.68	8.25	3.58	19.15	0.53	6.54	52.49	13.50	13.92	11.46
1967	4.85	7.06	3.37	17.68	0.54	6.64	52.24	13.17	13.89	12.02
1968	5.01	7.28	3.27	18.59	0.59	6.58	51.92	13.05	13.93	12.41
1969	5.12	7.62	3.46	19.12	0.62	6.79	49.31	12.25	14.11	13.01
1970	5.01	8.27	2.99	19.14	0.60	6.38	51.84	13.12	13.90	13.46
1971	5.59	8.70	3.12	20.07	0.90	6.66	49.18	13.39	14.56	12.67
1972	4.80	7.33	2.88	17.54	0.93	6.59	46.70	13.29	13.52	13.70
1973	5.24	7.32	2.95	17.90	1.30	7.06	45.93	12.48	13.93	14.30
1974	4.58	7.84	2.86	17.79	1.07	6.03	45.66	12.70	13.95	13.91
1975	4.92	7.50	2.87	17.51	1.33	6.43	43.90	11.58	13.78	14.72
1976	4.73	8.26	2.89	18.31	1.33	6.40	35.30	11.40	14.51	14.86
1977	4.90	7.24	2.96	17.50	1.43	6.02	40.79	12.15	14.71	14.55
1978	4.77	7.69	2.96	18.15	1.80	6.25	44.05	13.45	15.80	14.70
1979	5.01	8.84	2.88	19.62	2.20	6.38	43.59	10.88	15.48	16.04
1980	5.27	8.85	3.08	20.81	3.08	7.25	40.95	12.42	15.83	16.17
1981	4.97	8.44	3.12	19.95	3.99	7.92	41.87	11.98	15.74	17.01
1982	4.42	7.93	2.94	18.75	4.30	8.22	41.11	11.24	15.66	17.27
1983	4.79	8.11	2.86	19.64	5.20	9.05	39.88	10.78	15.71	17.37
1984	4.55	7.88	2.91	18.99	5.28	8.86	39.82	10.83	15.26	16.93
1985	4.08	7.98	2.81	18.52	5.21	8.54	40.96	9.78	15.70	18.48
1986	5.07	8.29	3.06	20.33	6.84	10.47	38.76	11.11	16.82	19.58
1987	4.81	8.12	3.21	20.25	7.17	10.76	37.68	9.97	16.67	19.47
1988	5.11	8.50	3.58	21.02	7.43	10.90	36.43	10.42	16.81	19.43
1989	5.18	8.46	4.00	21.45	7.52	10.95	35.59	10.23	17.13	19.06
1990	4.68	8.43	4.39	21.33	7.11	10.23	35.17	9.79	16.19	18.64

(c) Includes fruit juice.

Table 2 *continued*

CEREALS, SUGAR AND PRESERVES, AND BEVERAGES

ounces per person per week

	Bread	Flour	Cakes[(d)] and pastries	Biscuits[(e)]	Breakfast cereals	Total[(f)] cereals	Sugar	Preserves[(g)]	Tea	Coffee	Total beverages
1942	60.60	6.40		2.60	0.80	20.90	8.41	4.93			
1943	59.70	6.90		1.80	0.80	21.60	8.71	5.19			
1944	59.90	7.10		2.00	0.90	23.40	9.05	6.05			
1945	61.80	6.20		2.90	0.90	23.70	9.13	5.48			
1946	59.90	6.10		2.60	1.00	22.60	9.55	5.42			
1947	62.50	5.40		2.20	1.10	21.40	10.15	5.51			
1948	65.80	6.20		2.60	1.50	24.00	10.20	6.19			
1949	61.10	6.90		2.90	1.50	24.30	10.85	6.26			
1950	57.75	7.25	6.69	3.68	1.40	23.92	10.13	6.30	2.16	0.21	2.72
1951	58.22	8.12	6.48	4.64	1.44	25.66	11.44	5.91	2.01	0.38	2.78
1952	61.46	8.46	5.41	4.80	1.48	24.45	11.00	6.05	2.21	0.44	3.04
1953	57.56	8.75	5.94	5.10	1.55	25.21	13.57	5.10	2.65	0.35	3.41
1954	56.28	8.81	5.29	4.99	1.58	24.44	16.96	4.17	2.82	0.36	3.61
1955	55.13	8.57	5.56	5.12	1.69	24.91	17.64	4.09	2.79	0.36	3.54
1956	51.08	7.89	5.67	5.30	1.81	24.75	18.00	3.69	2.88	0.38	3.67
1957	48.00	7.81	5.83	5.50	1.82	25.12	17.70	3.59	2.81	0.40	3.61
1958	47.21	7.75	5.82	5.58	1.80	25.29	18.55	3.49	2.84	0.40	3.64
1959	47.29	6.74	5.99	5.60	1.74	24.49	18.50	3.30	2.80	0.39	3.54
1960	45.47	6.76	6.31	5.67	1.80	25.09	17.76	3.21	2.80	0.39	3.57
1961	45.17	6.37	6.09	5.60	1.90	24.37	18.10	3.03	2.84	0.38	3.60
1962	43.57	6.22	6.61	5.75	1.92	25.17	18.40	3.28	2.79	0.40	3.56
1963	43.26	6.51	6.57	5.58	1.94	25.15	18.49	3.16	2.82	0.44	3.66
1964	41.97	6.07	6.47	5.73	2.02	24.79	17.37	2.96	2.69	0.45	3.49
1965	40.60	6.09	6.73	5.83	1.97	25.73	17.56	2.99	2.61	0.44	3.44
1966	38.64	5.95	6.46	5.60	2.25	25.00	17.05	2.84	2.64	0.47	3.51
1967	40.02	5.79	6.04	5.87	2.35	25.05	17.21	2.85	2.70	0.48	3.56
1968	38.31	5.38	6.04	5.84	2.43	24.93	16.35	2.79	2.59	0.53	3.57
1969	37.74	5.38	5.86	5.81	2.63	24.86	16.18	2.67	2.52	0.58	3.56
1970	38.11	5.68	5.68	5.76	2.74	25.08	16.94	2.57	2.59	0.57	3.61
1971	35.76	5.86	5.46	5.80	2.68	25.01	15.80	2.71	2.39	0.60	3.36
1972	34.44	5.42	5.11	5.62	2.86	24.26	15.02	2.56	2.24	0.64	3.24
1973	33.42	5.25	4.81	5.82	2.95	24.57	13.69	2.51	2.16	0.61	3.09
1974	33.50	5.30	4.45	5.63	2.88	23.89	13.03	2.47	2.24	0.66	3.22
1975	33.67	5.16	4.24	5.60	3.05	23.51	11.29	2.43	2.18	0.65	3.11
1976	33.17	6.02	3.96	5.62	3.25	24.47	12.20	2.29	2.21	0.65	3.16
1977	32.73	6.46	3.87	5.62	3.30	24.81	12.09	2.36	2.07	0.48	2.88
1978	32.13	5.96	3.77	5.45	3.45	24.18	11.89	2.15	1.99	0.55	2.81
1979	31.38	5.75	4.01	5.54	3.38	24.43	11.55	2.17	2.11	0.62	3.06
1980	31.12	5.67	3.73	5.40	3.50	24.29	11.17	2.05	2.05	0.67	3.00
1981	31.23	5.96	3.77	5.39	3.53	24.54	11.08	2.08	1.98	0.65	2.95
1982	31.03	5.28	3.76	5.66	3.54	23.92	10.31	1.99	2.02	0.64	2.93
1983	30.74	4.97	3.59	5.47	3.83	23.95	9.84	2.05	2.04	0.69	3.02
1984	30.57	4.34	3.56	5.29	4.13	23.46	9.15	1.95	1.80	0.69	2.76
1985	30.99	4.05	3.49	5.22	4.04	22.85	8.41	1.87	1.74	0.68	2.70
1986	30.79	4.14	3.60	5.42	4.38	24.15	8.04	1.98	1.74	0.72	2.76
1987	30.60	3.93	3.70	5.32	4.42	24.27	7.48	1.88	1.71	0.67	2.70
1988	30.28	3.59	3.67	5.28	4.47	23.84	6.94	1.85	1.65	0.70	2.66
1989	29.43	3.28	3.60	5.26	4.45	23.90	6.46	1.76	1.61	0.65	2.60
1990	28.09	3.19	3.65	5.26	4.47	23.70	6.04	1.69	1.52	0.63	2.47

(d) Includes buns, scones and teacakes.
(e) Includes crispbread.
(f) Excludes bread.
(g) Includes honey and syrups.

Table 2 *continued*

	Fresh white fish	Fresh fat fish	Shell fish	Cooked fish	Total fish and fish products		Butter	Margarine	Lard	All other fats	Total fats
1942					6.61		1.98	4.15	1.78	0.73	8.64
1943					6.54		2.00	4.18	1.95	0.60	8.73
1944					7.62		2.05	4.29	1.98	0.88	9.20
1945					9.21		2.16	4.19	1.51	0.77	8.63
1946					10.55		2.83	3.46	1.17	0.77	8.23
1947					9.49		2.80	3.40	1.00	0.64	7.84
1948					9.96		3.20	3.90	1.06	0.72	8.88
1949					8.38		3.50	4.23	2.09	0.85	10.67
1950	3.13	0.56	0.12	1.02	6.62		4.56	3.94	1.96	1.15	11.61
1951	3.76	0.72	0.13	0.99	7.66		3.91	4.13	2.03	0.82	10.89
1952	3.77	0.65	0.09	1.10	7.52		2.79	4.39	2.01	0.59	9.78
1953	3.47	0.45	0.09	0.84	6.30		3.56	4.28	2.00	0.64	10.48
1954	3.12	0.41	0.08	0.67	5.68		4.09	4.81	2.18	0.59	11.67
1955	3.16	0.40	0.10	0.80	5.95		4.47	4.68	2.18	0.55	11.88
1956	3.10	0.37	0.12	0.89	6.13		4.70	4.48	2.08	0.58	11.84
1957	2.98	0.34	0.10	0.88	5.94		5.37	4.02	1.98	0.59	11.96
1958	2.63	0.31	0.12	0.97	5.70		6.10	3.46	2.15	0.53	12.24
1959	2.54	0.31	0.11	0.76	5.93		5.74	3.74	2.04	0.51	12.03
1960	2.37	0.31	0.09	0.86	5.86		5.68	3.66	2.06	0.57	11.97
1961	2.23	0.26	0.06	0.96	5.69		6.20	3.30	2.07	0.49	12.06
1962	2.42	0.25	0.06	0.89	5.79		6.20	3.15	2.14	0.50	11.99
1963	2.35	0.27	0.07	1.00	5.81		5.98	3.32	2.19	0.55	12.04
1964	2.23	0.28	0.07	1.00	5.94		5.98	3.35	2.12	0.58	12.03
1965	2.25	0.26	0.06	1.00	5.78		6.10	3.04	2.12	0.60	11.86
1966	2.18	0.24	0.06	1.02	5.79		6.09	2.79	2.13	0.62	11.63
1967	2.10	0.23	0.06	1.06	5.79		6.19	3.00	2.09	0.64	11.92
1968	1.99	0.21	0.06	1.07	5.69		6.14	2.81	2.08	0.74	11.77
1969	1.90	0.23	0.05	0.93	5.46		6.15	2.78	2.08	0.79	11.80
1970	1.75	0.21	0.04	1.01	5.35		5.99	2.86	2.21	0.89	11.95
1971	1.81	0.21	0.05	0.94	5.15		5.53	3.15	1.98	0.94	11.60
1972	1.51	0.18	0.05	1.04	5.05		4.79	3.52	1.89	0.92	11.12
1973	1.37	0.19	0.06	0.75	4.71		5.24	3.03	1.83	1.12	11.22
1974	1.27	0.17	0.06	0.74	4.33		5.61	2.60	1.82	1.02	11.04
1975	1.30	0.19	0.09	0.66	4.46		5.63	2.60	1.97	0.95	11.14
1976	1.22	0.17	0.08	0.66	4.58		5.16	3.06	1.86	0.90	10.98
1977	1.17	0.19	0.07	0.50	4.13		4.70	3.48	1.88	0.94	10.99
1978	1.18	0.17	0.09	0.64	4.25		4.55	3.54	1.91	1.14	11.14
1979	1.15	0.21	0.09	0.75	4.51		4.45	3.63	1.86	1.11	11.04
1980	1.13	0.24	0.11	0.74	4.80		4.05	3.83	1.81	1.54	11.22
1981	1.18	0.20	0.09	0.79	4.92		3.69	4.11	1.80	1.46	11.06
1982	1.08	0.20	0.12	0.82	5.04		3.17	4.33	1.76	1.72	10.98
1983	1.10	0.20	0.13	0.84	5.14		3.27	4.08	1.70	1.64	10.69
1984	1.05	0.22	0.13	0.70	4.89		2.87	4.08	1.51	1.83	10.29
1985	1.00	0.24	0.15	0.60	4.90		2.83	3.76	1.44	2.03	10.07
1986	1.04	0.25	0.17	0.63	5.16		2.27	4.10	1.36	2.76	10.49
1987	0.94	0.25	0.14	0.76	5.09		2.14	3.98	1.15	2.77	10.04
1988	0.97	0.23	0.17	0.65	5.06		2.00	3.78	1.00	3.07	9.86
1989	0.93	0.31	0.18	0.55	5.20		1.75	3.47	0.89	3.36	9.48
1990	0.87	0.27	0.18	0.54	5.08		1.61	3.19	0.80	3.39	9.00

Table 2 *continued*

ounces per person per week

	Beef and veal	Mutton and lamb	Pork	Bacon and ham	Poultry	Sausages	Total meat and meat products
1942	8.10	5.30	0.40	3.95		3.99	26.30
1943	7.20	6.00	1.00	4.03		3.78	26.20
1944	7.00	5.30	1.90	4.55		4.11	28.40
1945	6.30	6.10	1.40	3.54		3.87	26.30
1946	7.50	5.80	0.40	3.22		4.18	26.70
1947	6.30	5.80	0.10	1.95		4.30	25.50
1948	6.60	4.70	0.10	2.05		4.80	23.00
1949	6.50	4.80	0.10	2.68		4.19	22.70
1950	8.06	5.43	0.30	4.52	0.35	4.01	29.85
1951	6.23	3.45	0.36	4.63	0.57	3.55	31.96
1952	6.00	5.02	0.84	5.29	0.60	3.63	28.96
1953	8.08	6.18	1.60	5.96	0.60	3.50	32.34
1954	9.23	5.98	2.40	6.10	0.52	3.40	33.67
1955	9.36	6.55	2.32	6.08	0.48	3.48	34.42
1956	10.00	7.16	1.90	5.85	0.59	3.46	35.35
1957	10.54	6.28	1.98	5.87	0.80	3.54	35.44
1958	9.57	6.04	2.13	5.95	0.97	3.48	35.17
1959	8.55	6.97	2.01	5.97	1.35	3.52	35.18
1960	8.74	6.63	2.02	6.16	1.77	3.62	35.89
1961	9.10	6.75	1.95	6.16	2.42	3.59	36.76
1962	9.01	6.72	2.29	6.43	2.38	3.83	37.72
1963	9.47	6.36	2.48	6.23	2.59	3.75	38.10
1964	8.53	6.30	2.33	6.26	2.82	3.71	37.19
1965	8.08	5.90	2.80	6.32	3.51	3.73	37.60
1966	8.13	6.28	2.76	6.25	4.06	3.59	38.29
1967	8.61	6.06	2.29	6.13	4.01	3.50	38.29
1968	7.76	5.71	2.53	6.09	4.81	3.70	38.47
1969	7.70	5.34	2.78	6.05	4.93	3.68	38.50
1970	7.80	5.25	2.83	6.26	5.06	3.74	39.53
1971	7.96	5.41	3.04	6.04	4.92	3.69	39.01
1972	6.90	4.96	3.10	5.64	5.69	3.55	37.84
1973	6.31	4.44	3.00	5.34	6.09	3.41	36.63
1974	7.41	4.11	3.20	5.11	5.18	3.50	35.95
1975	8.32	4.25	2.73	4.99	5.73	3.22	37.12
1976	7.62	4.20	2.89	5.02	6.00	3.29	37.06
1977	8.25	3.97	3.32	5.37	6.17	3.47	38.58
1978	8.27	3.92	3.34	5.39	6.15	3.54	38.92
1979	8.27	4.28	3.63	5.46	6.82	3.49	40.27
1980	8.13	4.51	4.13	5.27	6.67	3.25	40.19
1981	6.96	4.25	3.82	5.27	7.30	3.41	39.34
1982	7.06	3.59	4.02	5.10	6.85	3.33	38.71
1983	6.57	3.87	3.53	5.11	6.99	3.33	38.13
1984	6.27	3.32	3.29	4.69	7.24	3.00	36.60
1985	6.51	3.27	3.45	4.83	6.90	2.97	36.77
1986	6.58	3.01	3.64	4.81	7.30	2.73	37.08
1987	6.77	2.65	3.17	4.61	8.14	2.66	36.97
1988	6.35	2.78	3.29	4.61	8.09	2.48	36.59
1989	6.03	2.99	3.15	4.57	7.76	2.53	35.94
1990	5.24	2.92	2.97	4.17	7.95	2.41	34.11

Table 3

Household food consumption by main food groups, according to region, for 1955 to 1990

ounces per person per week, except where otherwise stated

					Regions of England								
	England	Scotland	Wales	North[a]	Yorkhire and Humber-side[b]	North West	West[c] Midlands	East[d] Midlands	Eastern	South East and Southern	London	South[e] East and East Anglia	South West
MILK AND CREAM (pt or eq pt)													
1955	5.15	5.02	4.70	4.46[f]		5.19	5.36		5.04[g]	5.38	5.52		5.11
1960	5.15	5.05	4.56	4.24	4.93	5.13	5.33	5.09	5.32	5.43	5.47		5.37
1965	5.26	5.14	4.23	4.94	4.48	5.19	5.04	5.11	5.57	5.74	5.57		5.69
1970	5.02	4.76	4.84	4.33	4.70	5.05	5.05	5.27				5.41	5.36
1975	5.16	4.99	4.89	4.80	4.92	5.21	5.31	5.34				5.22	5.33
1980	4.55	4.70	4.89	4.10	4.37	4.55	4.55	4.75				4.59	4.82
1985	4.13	4.19	4.04	3.79	4.09	4.23	4.11	4.57				4.08	4.21
1990	3.81	3.80	3.83	3.67	4.01	3.68	3.61	4.18				3.77	4.03
CHEESE													
1955	3.00	2.39	2.71	1.98		2.43	3.46		2.86	3.58	2.96		3.75
1960	3.08	2.53	2.96	2.08	2.53	2.75	3.35	3.09	3.44	3.63	3.39		3.44
1965	3.27	2.98	2.98	2.40	2.47	2.86	3.94	3.11	3.67	3.72	3.52		3.74
1970	3.61	3.00	3.81	2.89	3.05	3.30	4.00	3.95				3.90	4.16
1975	3.76	3.59	3.26	2.98	3.06	3.48	4.48	4.15				3.98	4.20
1980	3.93	3.31	4.17	2.76	3.44	3.78	3.84	3.71				4.35	4.30
1985	3.95	3.67	3.79	3.16	3.14	3.82	4.40	4.21				4.08	4.59
1990	4.03	4.11	3.38	3.41	3.76	3.50	3.66	4.31				4.28	4.81
MEAT AND MEAT PRODUCTS													
1955	34.85	31.44	33.20	34.59		35.40	36.43		34.21	32.93	36.90		33.51
1960	36.01	33.54	35.79	38.05	35.84	36.44	39.21	34.00	32.29	34.63	37.78		35.81
1965	37.77	34.74	37.23	37.68	37.10	38.59	37.66	35.89	36.21	37.20	41.03		38.58
1970	40.02	35.09	41.20	43.02	38.50	40.07	41.00	39.05				39.17	39.30
1975	37.09	35.33	38.39	38.97	38.39	40.08	38.57	31.21				37.15	35.26
1980	40.15	42.36	37.26	44.27	37.11	40.90	42.70	35.20				40.73	37.65
1985	36.97	35.99	35.24	41.25	33.62	40.08	37.22	36.43				35.61	39.28
1990	33.95	34.48	35.92	35.63	34.44	33.05	36.02	33.62				33.21	34.33
FISH													
1955	5.81	5.99	6.34	6.54		6.29	4.87		5.54	5.70	6.61		5.13
1960	5.87	5.04	6.63	6.74	6.71	5.93	5.80	5.88	5.52	5.53	6.42		4.21
1965	5.86	5.26	5.50	6.92	7.08	5.80	5.07	5.53	5.96	5.13	5.92		5.31
1970	5.41	4.88	5.13	6.49	6.50	5.20	5.30	4.91				5.38	4.08
1975	4.53	3.99	3.97	5.50	5.34	4.20	4.43	3.94				4.58	3.70
1980	4.79	4.89	4.67	5.59	5.22	4.63	4.74	4.58				4.83	4.00
1985	4.93	5.04	4.24	5.59	5.28	4.69	4.53	4.57				4.93	5.02
1990	5.09	4.70	5.42	5.29	5.96	4.67	4.51	4.77				5.31	4.69

Table 3 *continued*

	England	Scotland	Wales	North[a]	Yorkshire and Humberside[b]	North West	West[c] Midlands	East[d] Midlands	Eastern	South East and Southern	London	South[e] East and East Anglia	South West
EGGS(no)													
1955	4.09	4.93	3.84	4.29[f]		4.04	3.72		4.10[g]	4.02	4.35		4.09
1960	4.63	5.01	4.41	4.92	4.94	4.22	4.28	4.46	4.45	4.86	4.72		4.80
1965	4.73	5.43	4.23	5.34	4.72	4.42	4.22	4.62	4.74	4.69	4.84		5.00
1970	4.72	4.83	4.64	5.46	4.62	4.22	4.33	4.92				4.54	4.95
1975	4.18	4.41	3.51	4.89	4.24	3.81	3.91	4.11				4.18	4.11
1980	3.67	3.81	3.74	4.17	3.99	3.49	3.59	3.55				3.52	3.88
1985	3.13	3.44	2.85	3.77	3.27	3.04	2.81	3.35				3.02	3.22
1990	2.17	2.61	2.14	2.89	2.38	2.28	1.90	2.19				1.98	2.30
FATS													
1955	11.93	10.68	13.52	12.76		12.12	11.65		12.20	11.72	10.84		12.22
1960	12.24	10.41	13.37	12.32	12.37	12.39	11.83	13.26	12.46	11.81	11.22		12.53
1965	11.91	11.33	13.16	12.03	13.00	11.99	11.22	12.32	11.95	11.37	11.24		12.11
1970	12.27	10.47	14.58	12.28	13.06	12.52	12.12	12.77				11.29	11.88
1975	11.46	10.00	12.17	12.06	11.75	10.93	11.78	11.00				10.67	12.03
1980	11.34	9.51	12.38	12.02	10.46	11.00	12.44	11.93				11.07	11.67
1985	10.17	9.01	10.31	10.43	10.01	10.29	10.45	11.16				9.84	10.19
1990	8.87	9.33	10.42	9.29	8.98	7.83	9.02	9.12				8.75	10.11
SUGAR AND PRESERVES													
1955	21.93	21.01	21.38	20.82		22.52	22.56		21.88	22.24	21.33		22.18
1960	20.98	20.36	22.16	17.15	19.77	22.13	22.88	22.64	22.73	21.42	20.20		19.86
1965	20.62	20.64	19.82	18.93	20.85	21.71	21.62	21.29	21.33	19.87	19.46		20.49
1970	19.59	17.48	22.32	17.66	20.42	20.28	21.00	20.96				18.79	17.99
1975	14.08	13.42	14.90	15.35	15.36	13.38	14.18	13.29				12.92	14.11
1980	13.15	13.54	13.90	12.98	12.51	13.84	15.24	14.10				12.06	14.28
1985	10.25	10.06	11.16	10.61	9.72	10.47	12.27	10.37				9.57	10.86
1990	7.58	8.57	8.49	9.17	7.32	7.49	8.36	7.02				7.12	8.21
VEGETABLES													
1955	98.87	90.50	98.75	91.72		95.43	105.97		96.67	94.79	101.00		106.44
1960	96.58	91.08	92.33	93.32	85.97	94.04	98.88	104.94	93.21	100.59	95.45		102.86
1965	92.74	88.82	111.99	95.13	96.54	89.13	96.95	91.53	90.21	88.93	90.69		95.53
1970	95.53	81.60	95.85	96.73	93.83	92.29	107.07	92.84				86.98	98.95
1975	84.70	75.73	95.70	91.04	86.63	82.66	79.97	82.69				84.89	85.03
1980	85.60	76.54	98.31	93.97	85.18	84.80	86.99	82.40				84.11	86.79
1985	86.10	74.18	85.44	90.61	88.93	85.71	86.39	86.58				82.90	90.67
1990	79.04	81.50	87.23	83.89	80.67	80.10	81.26	80.14				74.04	88.31

Regions of England

Table 3 *continued*

ounces per person per week, except where otherwise stated

Regions of England

	England	Scotland	Wales	North[a]	Yorkshire and Humberside[b]	North West	West[c] Midlands	East[d] Midlands	Eastern	South East and Southern	London	South[e] East and East Anglia	South West
FRUIT													
1955	22.55	16.57	21.33	21.21[f]		20.88	21.09	22.10[g]		23.50	27.10		21.94
1960	24.71	19.35	23.09	20.45	24.73	21.97	23.14	21.49	26.71	27.23	31.08		25.60
1965	26.59	19.39	21.92	23.75	23.10	22.72	26.16	25.19	29.65	30.00	31.95		26.82
1970	24.84	21.78	26.77	21.43	22.68	21.83	25.62	26.16				29.95	26.22
1975	23.36	20.64	19.55	20.26	18.76	24.41	24.50	20.63				27.02	27.97
1980	28.36	24.55	29.36	20.91	23.16	24.30	24.31	26.14				34.65	27.85
1985	27.71	23.87	23.03	23.02	23.76	22.91	21.38	27.93				32.72	30.76
1990	32.16	28.96	26.80	29.25	30.26	25.55	24.19	31.00				37.74	33.57
CEREALS													
1955	79.13	88.00	83.28	84.02		81.58	81.43	79.51		76.49	69.07		81.84
1960	70.91	77.17	73.71	77.78	68.82	72.01	70.42	76.89	69.26	68.88	62.26		71.78
1965	64.61	74.95	70.82	69.00	68.83	66.90	65.93	66.13	61.77	58.71	57.17		67.05
1970	64.39	67.14	67.59	69.72	68.37	65.06	65.05	64.40				56.66	61.49
1975	58.19	61.72	60.56	66.20	59.79	56.00	59.14	56.24				52.74	57.23
1980	54.94	60.09	55.27	64.06	52.82	55.78	62.09	55.90				50.83	55.87
1985	53.94	53.61	52.48	59.24	53.01	55.90	59.80	57.22				50.10	54.53
1990	51.06	58.51	52.75	56.79	53.20	48.08	53.35	50.79				49.55	52.36
BEVERAGES													
1955	3.67	2.80	3.39	3.37		3.66	3.92	3.56		3.74	3.76		3.65
1960	3.66	2.87	3.58	3.20	3.62	3.78	3.93	3.76	3.65	3.78	3.70		3.54
1965	3.54	2.83	3.46	3.23	3.40	3.54	3.69	3.51	3.65	3.46	3.60		3.82
1970	3.69	2.81	3.86	3.41	3.75	3.85	3.70	3.83				3.63	3.67
1975	3.21	2.49	3.12	3.50	3.12	2.99	3.28	2.86				3.16	3.54
1980	3.04	2.66	2.89	3.26	2.90	3.01	3.09	3.14				2.98	3.16
1985	2.76	2.30	2.69	2.88	2.53	2.67	2.91	2.84				2.73	2.74
1990	2.45	2.46	2.67	2.50	2.60	2.31	2.18	2.41				2.42	2.59

(a) Northern region included North Riding until 1974.
(b) East and West Ridings until 1974 including Lincolnshire (parts of Lindsey) from 1967.
(c) Midland until 1974.
(d) North Midland until 1974, including Rutland.
(e) Regional analyses have merged these areas since 1967 (Greater London results are shown in Type of Area Analysis).
(f) The Northern region and Ridings were merged until 1960.
(g) The Eastern region and North Midlands were merged until 1958.

Table 4
Household food consumption by main food groups, according to income group, for 1952 to 1990.

	Income groups[a]									
	Gross weekly income of head of household									
	Households with one or more earners						Households without an earner		OAP	ALL
	A1	A2	All A	B	C	D	E1	E2		
MILK AND CREAM (pt or eq pt)										
1952			6.18	5.26	4.88	4.71			4.82	5.08
1955	6.39	5.85	5.97	5.14	4.86	4.70		5.20	4.95	5.09
1960	6.23	5.74	5.86	5.22	4.92	4.57		5.21	4.98	5.14
1965	5.85	5.74	5.76	5.24	4.92	4.99		4.97	5.15	5.19
1970	5.97	5.58	5.69	5.14	4.86	4.46		4.80	5.26	5.08
1975	5.28	5.16	5.20	5.07	5.03	5.02	5.22	5.48	5.57	5.12
1980	4.71	4.66	4.67	4.52	4.43	4.42	5.33	4.94	5.09	4.58
1985	3.73	3.94	3.88	3.95	4.09	4.10	4.64	4.34	4.94	4.13
1990	3.63	3.72	3.68	3.70	3.74	3.87	4.72	4.00	4.31	3.82
CHEESE										
1952			2.29	2.10	2.21	2.12			2.01	2.17
1955	3.25	2.85	2.95	2.78	2.86	2.79		3.02	2.92	2.83
1960	4.14	3.20	3.42	2.92	3.09	2.67		3.52	3.24	3.04
1965	3.87	3.58	3.64	3.06	3.05	3.30		3.27	3.68	3.20
1970	4.68	4.02	4.21	3.54	3.47	3.00		3.22	3.91	3.59
1975	4.47	4.18	4.34	3.79	3.55	3.40	5.08	3.58	3.96	3.79
1980	5.30	4.56	4.76	4.06	3.58	3.15	4.90	3.78	3.68	3.89
1985	5.00	4.29	4.49	4.04	3.87	3.25	4.28	3.62	3.86	3.91
1990	4.81	4.77	4.78	4.17	3.75	3.46	5.05	3.53	3.50	4.00
MEAT AND MEAT PRODUCTS										
1952			30.20	28.80	28.86	29.55			27.77	28.99
1955	40.69	35.33	36.61	34.23	33.96	35.56		34.06	31.08	34.42
1960	44.75	36.54	38.44	35.80	36.02	32.81		35.63	33.64	35.89
1965	42.76	37.57	38.86	37.32	37.64	37.07		33.94	38.05	37.60
1970	48.10	39.43	41.90	40.24	38.73	37.65		34.20	41.07	39.53
1975	34.85	37.04	36.44	36.98	36.90	41.64	37.89	37.32	38.10	37.12
1980	43.63	43.06	43.12	39.24	39.76	39.20	47.02	40.09	41.43	40.19
1985	33.51	36.49	35.58	35.16	37.73	34.08	37.79	39.39	39.28	36.77
1990	32.58	30.40	31.29	34.41	34.55	33.80	38.36	34.10	33.31	34.11
FISH										
1952			9.42	7.40	7.10	8.02			7.48	7.52
1955	8.33	6.19	6.74	5.83	5.59	6.18		7.68	6.29	5.95
1960	7.28	6.18	6.42	5.73	5.66	5.71		7.28	6.38	5.86
1965	6.66	5.84	6.02	5.44	5.78	6.40		5.66	7.11	5.78
1970	5.96	5.26	5.46	5.14	5.19	5.57		6.07	6.75	5.35
1975	4.50	4.47	4.55	4.38	4.23	4.59	5.57	4.99	5.29	4.46
1980	4.14	4.50	4.39	4.52	4.76	4.93	6.30	5.32	5.97	4.80
1985	5.58	4.76	5.01	4.44	4.44	4.21	8.07	5.95	7.08	4.90
1990	5.44	4.47	4.87	4.82	4.54	4.67	8.80	5.69	6.65	5.08

Table 4 *continued*

	Income groups[a]									
	Gross weekly income of head of household									
	Households with one or more earners						Households without an earner		OAP	ALL
	A1	A2	All A	B	C	D	E1	E2		
EGGS (no)										
1952			3.63	2.96	2.93	2.68			2.39	2.95
1955	5.18	4.66	4.79	4.30	4.06	3.92		3.96	3.40	4.19
1960	5.66	5.16	5.28	4.66	4.54	4.24		4.64	4.20	4.64
1965	5.50	5.00	5.12	4.70	4.70	4.91		4.71	4.73	4.78
1970	5.10	4.86	4.93	5.14	5.19	4.36		4.29	4.95	4.66
1975	4.17	4.08	4.16	3.98	4.11	4.16	4.96	4.44	4.79	4.14
1980	3.80	3.59	3.65	3.37	3.67	3.99	4.54	4.21	4.45	3.69
1985	2.61	2.67	2.65	2.92	3.06	3.33	3.45	3.72	4.08	3.15
1990	1.98	1.84	1.90	1.85	2.27	2.61	2.78	2.65	3.13	2.20
FATS										
1952			9.85	9.83	9.75	9.67			9.85	9.78
1955	12.92	12.07	12.28	11.85	11.94	11.68		11.49	11.24	11.88
1960	12.43	11.74	11.90	12.10	11.92	11.30		12.27	12.00	11.97
1965	11.73	11.47	11.56	11.77	12.03	12.33		12.56	12.30	11.86
1970	12.19	10.98	11.34	11.80	12.12	10.73		10.94	14.15	11.95
1975	10.49	10.39	10.48	10.79	11.09	11.94	13.76	11.46	13.06	11.14
1980	9.51	10.52	10.23	10.39	11.25	11.79	14.28	13.23	14.00	11.22
1985	8.92	8.68	8.76	9.07	10.13	9.47	12.29	11.72	13.51	10.07
1990	7.18	7.88	7.60	8.41	8.77	8.81	10.33	10.82	12.34	9.00
SUGAR AND PRESERVES										
1952			17.68	17.05	17.08	16.60			17.22	17.05
1955	21.85	21.91	21.90	21.54	21.87	21.07		23.62	22.80	21.73
1960	21.21	19.55	19.96	21.13	20.67	21.21		22.60	23.37	20.97
1965	17.76	19.12	18.78	19.88	21.28	22.46		22.25	24.00	20.55
1970	17.41	16.60	16.86	18.59	19.88	19.78		19.81	24.91	19.51
1975	8.80	11.38	10.62	12.68	14.42	14.91	14.28	17.04	19.46	13.72
1980	9.73	11.45	10.95	11.20	13.22	13.80	18.50	17.44	21.34	13.22
1985	7.89	7.72	7.72	8.16	10.17	11.35	12.52	12.86	17.30	10.27
1990	4.99	5.76	5.44	6.14	7.64	9.22	11.77	10.18	14.08	7.73
VEGETABLES[b]										
1952			88.98	100.06	101.26	97.20			85.45	98.57
1955	80.51	87.89	85.95	93.50	94.01	92.94		77.70	73.56	91.83
1960	79.63	84.46	83.38	91.35	92.48	91.10		94.39	78.56	90.31
1965	79.95	80.08	80.31	89.27	92.06	98.19		75.61	77.90	88.04
1970	77.44	76.79	76.89	87.08	91.58	90.09		84.95	79.34	87.55
1975	73.25	78.26	76.99	83.34	87.03	90.23	86.37	80.41	81.14	83.98
1980	83.24	77.75	79.40	81.38	88.96	90.76	88.68	88.88	89.13	85.37
1985	72.86	71.93	72.41	98.75	86.31	96.45	89.10	92.95	87.57	84.92
1990	68.52	67.51	67.92	75.55	81.54	82.77	95.41	93.41	82.82	79.79

Table 4 *continued*

	Income groups[a]										
	Gross weekly income of head of household										
	Households with one or more earners						Households without an earner		OAP	ALL
	A1	A2	All A	B	C	D	E1	E2		
FRUIT[b]										
1952			40.66	28.25	22.16	21.77			17.28	25.39
1955	43.38	36.67	38.32	28.44	23.84	23.76		27.34	17.00	27.14
1960	50.47	39.50	42.09	30.76	26.28	22.27		31.61	24.21	29.75
1965	51.15	39.48	42.37	30.54	25.39	24.48		27.17	25.97	30.14
1970	51.98	41.76	44.84	31.67	25.94	22.11		27.28	30.41	30.34
1975	34.99	30.61	32.19	23.74	19.86	19.03	40.02	28.80	26.28	23.94
1980	43.72	36.87	38.68	29.03	24.09	19.92	44.87	30.30	27.03	28.06
1985	45.56	36.98	39.54	29.45	23.02	16.13	46.19	23.37	29.24	27.06
1990	42.90	42.28	42.55	32.90	26.31	20.60	53.45	28.50	31.00	31.56
CEREALS										
1952			74.15	83.05	89.90	88.40			83.85	85.91
1955	67.01	75.20	73.09	78.60	83.89	82.79		76.15	76.98	80.04
1960	58.60	63.83	62.64	69.66	73.69	73.77		70.25	70.74	70.56
1965	52.13	58.59	57.03	64.78	69.65	73.44		66.82	69.30	65.79
1970	50.44	55.01	53.71	61.61	66.25	65.34		62.48	69.60	63.19
1975	47.92	50.27	49.64	55.97	59.55	60.29	57.56	61.91	62.18	57.18
1980	46.01	49.43	48.46	53.10	57.47	56.96	57.88	60.28	63.30	55.41
1985	44.92	45.09	45.12	50.51	54.80	56.30	58.04	59.31	62.73	53.84
1990	43.00	47.01	45.41	50.43	52.11	53.79	58.04	55.41	58.00	51.79
BEVERAGES										
1952			3.39	2.88	2.93	3.32			3.83	3.04
1955	3.94	3.43	3.55	3.43	3.53	3.78		3.84	4.21	3.54
1960	3.78	3.27	3.40	3.51	3.54	3.84		4.29	4.48	3.57
1965	3.47	3.19	3.26	3.21	3.52	3.88		3.89	4.77	3.44
1970	3.22	3.15	3.18	3.45	3.52	3.70		3.75	5.63	3.61
1975	2.41	2.58	2.54	2.88	2.98	3.44	3.97	4.61	4.85	3.11
1980	2.30	2.66	2.56	2.56	2.97	3.24	4.49	4.01	4.64	3.00
1985	2.23	2.22	2.21	2.28	2.60	2.63	4.29	3.40	4.17	2.70
1990	2.16	2.14	2.17	2.09	2.31	2.65	3.67	3.23	3.90	2.47

(a) Income group definitions vary over time. In particular, up to and including 1974, groups A, B and C included non - earners
In 1952 group D also included non - earners.
(b) Tomatoes are included with Fruit prior to 1975.

Table 5

Household food expenditure by main food groups, according to income group, for 1952 to 1990

pence per person per week

	Income group[a]									
	Gross weekly income of head of household									
	Households with one or more earners						Households without an earner		OAP	ALL
	A1	A2	All A	B	C	D	E1	E2		
MILK AND CREAM										
1952			13.27	11.47	10.67	11.66			12.88	11.35
1955	17.26	14.38	15.13	12.74	11.75	12.83		15.09	14.55	12.83
1960	19.35	16.91	17.48	15.60	14.47	13.56		17.25	16.53	15.38
1965	24.12	20.54	21.42	17.94	16.69	17.38		17.70	20.33	18.19
1970	30.26	25.71	27.06	22.16	20.97	19.63		20.46	25.56	22.34
1975	41.02	36.86	38.36	35.33	34.07	35.23	38.84	38.08	39.07	35.75
1980	88.19	86.25	86.73	79.82	76.55	72.95	102.68	84.20	87.59	80.24
1985	101.54	101.42	101.66	97.48	96.99	90.61	116.51	95.20	115.63	98.66
1990	137.94	135.04	136.16	127.64	123.01	118.59	160.95	121.34	135.16	127.69
CHEESE										
1952			2.13	1.82	1.85	1.75			1.58	1.84
1955	3.28	2.53	2.72	2.42	2.41	2.34		2.64	2.48	2.45
1960	4.89	3.53	3.85	3.14	3.28	2.84		3.68	3.44	3.27
1965	5.17	4.30	4.51	3.59	3.57	3.92		3.96	4.25	3.79
1970	6.94	5.40	5.85	4.58	4.50	3.86		4.05	5.04	4.68
1975	13.88	11.37	12.34	10.24	9.64	9.22	14.82	10.10	10.93	10.38
1980	34.83	29.15	30.68	24.63	21.68	19.12	30.42	23.09	22.47	23.83
1985	45.74	36.58	39.19	32.50	29.79	25.51	37.99	28.46	31.22	31.32
1990	55.95	52.87	53.97	43.08	37.92	32.43	55.81	36.10	35.22	41.43
MEAT AND MEAT PRODUCTS										
1952			27.77	25.43	24.55	24.80			22.09	25.06
1955	46.53	37.66	39.86	35.40	34.41	35.65		33.51	29.20	35.30
1960	57.70	44.49	47.60	42.31	41.55	37.20		39.91	38.03	42.11
1965	52.40	54.84	62.27	50.22	49.95	49.83		45.91	49.72	50.70
1970	87.21	68.35	73.76	64.54	62.47	59.44		52.53	66.13	64.61
1975	122.39	123.09	123.09	117.41	114.77	126.28	125.85	118.32	121.23	117.95
1980	262.90	263.29	262.95	224.00	224.41	217.91	282.42	229.15	236.04	230.48
1985	296.28	286.98	289.76	266.86	274.19	233.04	322.05	219.30	298.22	273.51
1990	374.79	340.39	354.15	344.13	335.61	299.33	394.94	311.81	318.02	337.24
FISH										
1952			7.23	5.07	4.71	5.15			4.56	5.09
1955	7.88	5.15	5.83	4.68	4.36	4.79		5.52	4.25	4.71
1960	9.56	7.46	7.96	6.53	6.13	6.08		6.84	6.23	6.53
1965	9.46	8.15	8.46	7.37	7.63	8.21		7.29	8.92	7.73
1970	11.86	8.98	9.82	8.65	8.61	8.82		10.00	10.52	8.93
1975	16.54	16.05	16.47	15.59	14.57	16.18	20.65	17.22	18.03	15.72
1980	30.32	32.69	32.00	30.35	31.51	31.31	42.30	34.05	40.49	32.12
1985	68.72	46.36	52.96	41.73	39.18	35.82	75.36	50.82	60.17	44.54
1990	91.98	67.42	77.38	63.71	56.93	56.33	120.20	70.43	81.36	66.62

Table 5 *continued*

	A1	A2	All A	B	C	D	E1	E2	OAP	ALL
Income group[a]										
Gross weekly income of head of household										
Households with one or more earners							Households without an earner		OAP	ALL
EGGS										
1952			5.10	5.06	4.68	4.54			4.18	4.80
1955	8.61	7.70	7.96	7.60	6.82	6.87		7.14	5.80	7.23
1960	8.97	8.43	8.56	7.85	7.40	7.13		7.57	7.11	7.69
1965	9.20	7.74	8.11	7.41	7.18	7.21		7.82	7.56	7.45
1970	9.20	8.30	8.55	8.16	7.91	7.74		7.78	9.02	8.15
1975	12.84	12.21	12.56	11.99	12.23	13.14	15.15	14.03	15.22	12.54
1980	19.91	19.28	19.46	17.47	18.72	20.92	24.15	22.75	23.74	19.22
1985	19.49	18.60	18.81	19.39	20.66	21.35	24.55	24.18	27.73	21.10
1990	18.44	17.99	18.25	16.55	19.56	21.93	26.36	22.73	28.05	19.49
FATS										
1952			5.31	5.23	5.17	5.13			5.20	5.18
1955	11.30	10.90	10.37	9.48	9.18	9.23		9.65	9.31	9,46
1960	10.90	9.70	9.98	9.60	9.12	8.62		9.98	9.79	9.44
1965	11.74	10.49	10.80	10.28	10.30	10.64		11.43	11.50	10.45
1970	12.13	10.54	10.99	10.50	10.54	9.17		9.77	13.06	10.65
1975	17.87	17.24	17.58	17.51	17.84	18.89	23.48	19.05	21.73	18.13
1980	31.47	33.24	32.75	30.54	32.44	32.90	47.62	39.33	41.59	33.15
1985	36.73	35.05	35.66	33.50	36.01	31.06	49.19	42.17	51.06	36.77
1990	35.64	34.77	35.07	33.84	34.44	32.32	45.51	40.82	49.96	36.11
SUGAR AND PRESERVES										
1952			4.45	4.23	4.26	4.07			4.39	4.24
1955	5.63	5.53	5.57	5.27	5.37	5.15		5.93	5.55	5.35
1960	6.12	5.11	5.35	5.27	5.16	5.27		5.86	6.01	5.28
1965	5.80	5.75	5.75	5.65	5.95	6.32		6.81	6.93	5.89
1970	5.85	5.41	5.54	5.45	5.75	5.53		5.95	7.61	5.74
1975	9.50	11.23	10.75	11.73	13.26	13.83	14.87	16.72	19.69	12.94
1980	13.80	15.55	15.04	13.90	15.75	16.21	24.53	22.00	27.07	16.38
1985	16.96	13.98	14.77	14.15	16.52	17.95	23.76	21.81	29.13	17.36
1990	13.99	15.36	14.75	14.90	16.67	19.94	30.11	22.87	33.49	18.08
VEGETABLES[b]										
1952			10.85	11.22	10.45	10.16			7.98	10.59
1955	11.74	11.55	11.60	11.90	10.60	11.46		9.19	7.82	11.23
1960	14.18	13.48	13.67	13.51	12.56	11.86		11.73	9.91	12.92
1965	17.71	15.96	16.41	16.10	15.15	15.87		13.66	12.24	15.51
1970	24.00	20.68	21.67	22.04	21.65	21.80		19.85	18.42	21.63
1975	50.48	47.40	48.28	49.91	49.23	50.36	48.72	48.24	43.32	49.14
1980	87.48	84.18	85.22	80.39	80.19	86.73	87.12	78.99	73.03	80.22
1985	135.48	114.54	120.97	115.75	113.35	104.44	122.80	108.69	103.17	113.04
1990	190.76	185.68	187.53	179.25	162.11	153.01	180.75	160.09	135.66	169.45

Table 5 *continued*

	Income group[a]									
	Gross weekly income of head of household									
	Households with one or more earners						Households without an earner		OAP	ALL
	A1	A2	All A	B	C	D	E1	E2		
FRUIT[b]										
1952			13.48	9.60	7.23	6.81			4.96	8.35
1955	16.85	14.16	14.83	11.02	9.09	9.06		9.58	5.71	10.38
1960	19.94	15.48	16.53	12.19	10.44	8.65		10.65	8.84	11.69
1965	23.60	17.74	19.15	14.01	11.72	11.48		12.63	11.58	13.78
1970	27.86	21.60	23.48	16.45	13.62	11.74		13.55	15.05	15.71
1975	37.70	29.63	32.32	22.67	18.84	17.66	36.27	26.73	23.72	22.84
1980	70.76	60.07	62.90	44.65	38.23	30.83	72.19	46.64	39.89	43.91
1985	115.73	83.61	93.42	65.57	50.70	35.96	105.54	51.45	62.90	60.39
1990	142.73	142.28	142.60	101.97	78.94	61.39	160.38	83.59	90.76	97.13
CEREALS										
1952			19.85	19.58	19.56	18.65			16.73	19.35
1955	19.14	19.89	19.65	19.32	19.58	18.35		18.03	16.49	19.17
1960	22.44	22.53	22.52	22.70	23.12	21.88		22.03	21.35	22.70
1965	24.47	24.70	24.64	26.06	26.85	27.53		25.99	26.64	26.18
1970	29.29	31.13	30.58	32.07	33.06	30.91		29.31	34.05	32.20
1975	57.58	53.25	54.55	56.36	57.94	58.35	57.41	63.14	62.61	57.37
1980	105.11	110.63	108.99	107.07	111.83	104.28	118.23	114.86	117.49	109.85
1985	142.43	142.51	142.84	141.02	144.50	129.71	170.93	147.56	158.72	144.12
1990	204.01	216.06	211.33	211.44	196.46	185.59	224.06	191.91	202.46	203.98
BEVERAGES										
1952			5.25	4.11	4.05	4.65			5.30	4.30
1955	9.16	7.72	8.09	7.27	7.39	7.88		8.44	8.68	7.53
1960	8.98	7.45	7.82	7.43	7.27	7.66		8.98	9.13	7.54
1965	0.56	7.50	7.77	7.03	7.43	8.00		8.55	9.83	7.50
1970	9.07	9.03	9.04	8.62	8.40	8.76		8.73	12.49	8.88
1975	11.63	11.08	11.28	10.86	10.87	12.35	16.92	16.33	15.55	11.57
1980	28.42	29.52	29.25	24.93	26.36	27.72	43.92	34.84	34.99	27.69
1985	43.25	39.25	40.18	37.72	39.89	37.57	69.05	46.64	55.87	41.57
1990	42.01	38.43	40.01	39.02	40.68	42.79	63.72	51.74	60.26	43.18
TOTAL										
1952			119.51	106.10	99.87	99.80			92.13	103.16
1955	161.35	139.99	145.30	129.83	123.56	125.80		127.08	111.71	128.36
1960	188.41	159.01	165.97	149.96	143.91	133.75		148.20	139.27	148.24
1965	208.57	180.78	187.67	170.89	167.20	170.52		166.24	173.73	172.28
1970	263	224	235	211	204	193		188	222	211
1975	405	385	392	373	365	383	428	400	402	377
1980	804	792	795	702	702	674	904	752	764	721
1985	1064	953	987	900	897	794	1162	926	1029	917
1990	1374	1308	1334	1230	1150	1067	1527	1160	1213	1212

(a) Income group definitions vary over time. In particular, up to and including 1974, groups A, B and C included non - earners.
   In 1952 group D also included non - earners.
(b) Tomatoes are included with Fruit prior to 1975.

Table 6

Household food consumption by main food groups according to household composition, 1952 to 1990

					Households with				
No. of adults	1	2	3	4 or more	2[a]				
No. of children		0			0[b]	1	2	3	4 or more
MILK AND CREAM (pt or eq pt)									
1952					5.94	5.76	5.38	5.12	4.75
1955					5.61	5.58	5.40	5.11	4.57
1960					5.44	5.41	5.40	5.26	4.64
1965					5.52	5.68	5.55	5.39	4.87
1970					5.52	5.31	5.29	4.99	4.74
1975	6.16	5.28	5.16	4.67	5.28	5.43	5.16	4.81	4.66
1980	5.56	4.81	4.47	4.33	4.81	4.72	4.50	4.33	4.15
1985	5.14	4.36	4.07	4.05	4.36	4.12	3.99	3.72	3.76
1990	4.55	4.07	3.85	3.60	4.07	3.94	3.58	3.40	3.48
CHEESE									
1952					2.88	2.11	1.86	1.65	1.52
1955					3.87	2.86	2.35	2.09	1.61
1960					4.16	3.07	2.45	2.12	1.81
1965					4.42	2.99	2.70	2.16	1.82
1970					5.27	3.66	3.02	2.59	1.93
1975	5.31	4.78	4.59	4.28	4.78	3.71	3.21	2.74	2.63
1980	4.69	4.78	4.48	4.10	4.78	3.70	3.64	3.02	2.52
1985	4.68	4.77	4.47	3.90	4.77	4.01	3.42	2.90	2.57
1990	4.64	4.78	4.37	4.45	4.78	3.70	3.65	2.94	2.87
MEAT AND MEAT PRODUCTS									
1952					39.84	29.44	25.25	22.35	19.84
1955					47.70	34.82	28.46	25.04	21.29
1960					48.01	36.77	29.99	25.31	22.31
1965					50.82	39.06	31.66	27.21	23.78
1970					52.71	39.77	32.14	28.83	27.05
1975	40.66	46.76	45.49	40.90	46.76	37.02	31.50	31.31	26.67
1980	42.61	48.74	48.76	42.14	48.74	42.17	33.99	31.59	27.12
1985	39.13	44.01	45.42	39.81	44.01	34.26	31.65	28.44	22.82
1990	35.09	40.48	41.51	37.72	40.48	34.75	27.63	26.62	27.43
FISH									
1952					11.66	7.02	5.48	4.75	4.30
1955					7.62	5.66	4.49	4.39	3.40
1960					7.39	5.61	4.55	3.79	3.23
1965					7.43	5.89	4.56	3.88	3.36
1970					6.66	5.38	4.15	3.87	3.24
1975	5.62	5.90	5.53	5.23	5.90	4.35	3.52	3.26	2.87
1980	6.20	6.48	5.58	5.47	6.48	4.54	3.87	3.26	2.98
1985	7.39	6.87	6.37	5.09	6.87	3.88	3.83	3.19	2.19
1990	6.82	7.13	5.59	5.19	7.13	4.61	3.66	3.09	3.04

Table 6 *continued*

	Households with								
No. of adults	1	2	3	4 or more	2[a]				
No. of children	0				0[b]	1	2	3	4 or more
EGGS (no)									
1952					3.73	3.12	2.86	2.63	2.52
1955					5.65	4.44	3.89	3.58	2.95
1960					5.62	4.87	4.29	3.87	3.56
1965					5.88	4.60	4.40	4.00	3.76
1970					5.48	4.66	4.11	3.87	3.66
1975	5.52	4.75	4.76	4.53	4.75	4.01	3.66	3.44	3.47
1980	4.69	4.39	3.86	3.96	4.39	3.45	3.16	3.18	3.16
1985	3.98	3.75	3.69	3.40	3.75	2.93	2.51	2.71	2.32
1990	2.97	2.71	2.58	2.12	2.71	2.02	1.62	1.75	1.79
FATS									
1952					10.51	9.68	9.47	9.50	9.41
1955					15.01	12.35	10.67	9.83	9.22
1960					14.89	12.31	10.52	9.37	9.41
1965					14.89	11.96	10.60	9.55	8.79
1970					14.97	11.71	10.33	10.46	8.81
1975	13.19	13.37	12.70	11.98	13.37	11.42	9.58	9.10	8.97
1980	13.46	13.73	12.51	11.18	13.73	10.75	9.13	9.00	9.66
1985	12.31	12.66	11.13	11.02	12.66	9.08	8.15	7.99	6.84
1990	10.76	11.40	9.78	11.01	11.40	7.98	6.94	6.56	7.07
SUGAR AND PRESERVES									
1952					19.32	17.37	16.78	15.98	15.91
1955					26.17	22.10	20.16	19.70	18.65
1960					24.70	21.22	18.71	18.30	17.73
1965					22.90	19.94	18.10	17.12	17.15
1970					22.20	18.48	15.96	16.21	16.65
1975	20.17	15.82	15.42	13.78	15.82	13.23	11.48	11.37	12.83
1980	18.40	17.25	14.24	12.05	17.25	11.36	10.44	10.63	13.76
1985	14.34	12.90	11.74	9.91	12.90	8.43	7.93	8.14	8.54
1990	11.86	9.93	8.01	8.30	9.93	6.83	5.49	5.66	6.68
VEGETABLES[c]									
1952					118.40	102.25	88.01	87.70	88.53
1955					113.67	96.50	84.81	84.95	78.11
1960					106.31	91.75	86.95	77.42	77.85
1965					99.66	88.43	78.75	77.97	75.11
1970					113.62	84.91	77.42	78.05	74.88
1975	84.39	92.29	94.25	89.96	92.29	84.39	73.96	76.65	80.51
1980	88.15	95.73	92.36	85.90	95.73	85.11	77.82	76.83	81.69
1985	83.67	98.25	97.25	84.58	98.25	83.69	75.11	70.95	78.11
1990	77.38	96.83	93.10	84.79	96.83	78.47	63.41	65.59	68.28

Table 6 *continued*

ounces per person per week, except where otherwise stated

		Households with								
No. of adults	1	2	3	4 or more	2[a]					
No. of children		0			0[b]	1	2	3	4 or more	

FRUIT[c]									
1952					36.82	28.43	23.99	18.33	14.75
1955					39.82	30.89	25.46	20.75	16.16
1960					43.59	31.52	26.48	21.08	17.48
1965					40.79	33.03	27.37	22.50	15.96
1970					40.20	30.45	26.88	25.82	20.33
1975	35.54	30.88	29.26	23.68	30.88	24.41	20.19	18.58	14.98
1980	35.42	34.99	28.62	28.72	34.99	27.90	25.48	22.87	21.16
1985	37.71	35.01	28.29	23.21	35.01	25.83	24.55	19.65	16.56
1990	40.90	39.81	32.09	30.63	39.81	30.87	27.72	22.40	20.67

CEREALS									
1952					101.42	84.07	73.67	72.79	77.34
1955					95.73	77.57	70.20	68.16	69.74
1960					81.04	70.06	63.51	59.05	62.56
1965					77.14	63.17	57.42	55.65	57.66
1970					70.84	60.91	55.06	55.76	56.63
1975	64.34	62.22	61.19	56.10	62.22	56.69	52.13	53.33	55.21
1980	62.30	60.48	56.08	51.21	60.48	56.15	49.89	51.93	55.37
1985	63.13	58.98	55.92	54.13	58.98	52.01	48.67	47.17	47.11
1990	60.81	56.32	55.11	53.90	56.32	49.51	47.77	44.18	51.12

BEVERAGES									
1952					4.14	2.92	2.56	2.30	2.02
1955					4.98	3.61	2.87	2.50	2.18
1960					4.71	3.55	2.87	2.62	2.25
1965					4.54	3.39	2.64	2.40	2.10
1970					4.73	3.32	2.71	2.30	2.21
1975	5.43	4.25	3.86	3.53	4.25	2.77	2.27	2.12	2.06
1980	4.99	4.24	3.90	3.01	4.24	2.82	2.06	1.88	1.85
1985	4.14	3.76	3.30	2.82	3.76	2.54	1.88	1.73	1.12
1990	3.85	3.34	2.62	2.49	3.34	2.20	1.71	1.70	1.63

(a) Until 1970, data shown relate to households containing one adult of each sex and excludes households containing adolescents (aged 15 - 17 years)
(b) Until 1970, includes only households where both adults are aged under 55.
(c) Tomatoes are included with Fruit prior to 1975.

Table 7

Household food expenditure by main food groups, according to household composition, 1952 to 1990

pence per person per week

						Households with				
No. of adults	1	2	3	4 or more		2[a]				
No. of children		0				0[b]	1	2	3	4 or more
MILK AND CREAM										
1952						15.32	12.23	10.20	8.68	7.23
1955						16.56	13.68	11.61	10.10	7.85
1960						18.75	15.86	14.63	13.11	10.68
1965						21.73	19.05	16.98	15.75	12.95
1970						27.66	22.09	20.77	18.53	17.34
1975	45.56	38.38	37.20	32.17		38.38	38.46	35.14	31.85	30.85
1980	98.72	86.98	80.50	75.38		86.98	84.57	77.33	74.70	67.95
1985	124.14	107.12	98.81	94.28		107.12	101.03	94.37	87.09	82.69
1990	153.94	138.26	128.44	114.95		138.26	135.56	123.31	108.17	110.56
CHEESE										
1952						2.65	1.81	1.58	1.30	1.13
1955						3.48	2.50	2.03	1.80	1.36
1960						4.59	3.34	2.66	2.24	1.90
1965						5.28	3.58	3.22	2.56	2.12
1970						6.98	4.72	3.93	3.32	2.52
1975	14.71	13.26	12.62	11.94		13.26	10.23	8.68	7.44	6.90
1980	29.36	29.70	27.68	24.96		29.70	22.94	21.99	18.22	15.23
1985	38.78	39.04	35.94	30.56		39.04	32.02	27.31	22.55	19.49
1990	49.84	50.73	45.08	45.45		50.73	37.73	37.26	29.01	28.04
MEAT AND MEAT PRODUCTS										
1952						35.70	26.01	22.03	18.95	16.76
1955						52.45	36.53	28.93	24.68	20.46
1960						61.09	43.06	34.45	28.12	24.00
1965						72.11	52.66	41.88	34.90	29.16
1970						91.11	65.22	51.60	45.25	41.05
1975	134.92	155.07	152.97	129.75		155.07	118.05	97.56	91.03	74.55
1980	252.89	291.23	290.40	253.92		291.23	251.05	185.99	169.88	136.15
1985	304.41	344.01	345.59	312.62		344.01	257.16	228.03	197.88	148.52
1990	362.53	416.11	412.81	391.69		416.11	355.39	262.12	229.71	211.49
FISH										
1952						8.20	4.97	3.85	3.21	2.81
1955						6.80	4.68	3.49	3.28	2.70
1960						9.62	6.46	5.05	4.02	3.38
1965						10.96	8.24	6.06	5.06	4.04
1970						12.71	8.98	6.77	6.24	5.36
1975	20.11	21.54	19.64	19.02		21.54	15.29	12.17	10.97	9.59
1980	42.76	44.04	38.75	35.38		44.04	31.18	25.62	20.78	17.32
1985	67.59	64.26	59.62	47.31		64.26	35.30	33.94	26.72	19.90
1990	94.02	94.32	75.62	69.08		94.32	60.75	46.72	37.35	37.92

Table 7 *continued*

pence per person per week

					Households with				
No. of adults	1	2	3	4 or more	2[a]				
No. of children		0			0[b]	1	2	3	4 or more
EGGS									
1952					5.87	5.13	4.96	4.46	4.21
1955					10.32	8.01	6.81	6.27	4.76
1960					9.79	8.08	7.14	6.33	5.55
1965					9.73	7.08	6.83	6.17	5.65
1970					10.01	8.08	6.99	6.60	6.36
1975	17.87	14.81	14.93	12.86	14.81	12.10	10.82	10.17	9.89
1980	25.98	23.45	20.15	21.15	23.45	17.98	16.13	16.04	15.77
1985	28.92	25.59	24.06	22.22	25.59	19.89	16.60	17.57	13.87
1990	28.57	24.72	21.98	17.21	24.72	17.78	14.55	14.63	14.84
FATS									
1952					5.64	5.11	5.03	5.04	4.84
1955					12.96	9.87	8.26	7.40	6.48
1960					12.38	9.66	8.06	6.96	6.63
1965					13.75	10.40	9.23	8.04	6.90
1970					13.54	10.37	8.92	8.78	7.32
1975	22.70	22.25	20.83	19.16	22.25	18.48	15.55	14.37	14.21
1980	43.11	42.33	38.55	34.48	42.33	31.40	25.83	24.72	26.83
1985	49.28	47.84	41.77	40.80	47.84	32.02	29.16	26.27	21.53
1990	46.09	46.71	42.17	40.74	46.71	32.10	27.75	25.12	22.88
SUGAR AND PRESERVES									
1952					4.99	4.37	4.12	3.85	3.73
1955					6.48	5.46	4.95	4.88	4.65
1960					6.25	5.33	4.60	4.58	4.47
1965					6.66	5.57	5.05	4.88	4.90
1970					6.90	5.46	4.59	4.54	4.70
1975	20.37	15.06	14.50	12.38	15.60	12.21	10.56	10.51	11.80
1980	24.54	21.81	17.28	14.67	21.81	14.27	12.86	12.72	15.98
1985	26.86	22.55	19.54	15.84	22.55	14.26	13.29	13.28	13.10
1990	30.18	23.37	19.42	18.65	23.37	15.51	12.86	12.57	14.44
VEGETABLES[c]									
1952					14.78	11.32	9.73	8.95	8.39
1955					15.55	12.47	10.43	9.69	8.85
1960					17.70	13.58	12.24	10.34	9.73
1965					20.75	16.88	14.06	13.25	11.85
1970					30.32	23.13	19.63	18.18	16.68
1975	55.18	55.28	53.57	47.98	55.28	52.60	44.02	41.45	42.42
1980	90.99	91.79	80.49	84.42	91.79	83.09	74.03	68.25	69.82
1985	129.70	131.41	119.73	102.68	131.41	116.63	105.51	89.62	81.18
1990	188.69	195.93	184.80	172.23	195.93	182.53	147.55	132.31	134.21

Table 7 *continued*

					Households with				
No. of adults	1	2	3	4 or more		2[a]			
No. of children		0			0[b]	1	2	3	4 or more
FRUIT[c]									
1952					12.96	10.12	8.09	5.88	4.78
1955					16.01	12.29	9.64	7.68	6.08
1960					17.64	12.83	10.24	8.16	6.63
1965					19.68	15.60	12.52	10.33	6.91
1970					22.54	16.38	14.10	12.73	10.05
1975	33.78	29.07	27.57	21.58	29.07	24.54	19.29	17.16	13.80
1980	56.00	55.42	44.47	48.13	55.42	45.52	38.72	35.40	29.79
1985	88.02	79.01	63.20	49.90	79.01	59.94	54.37	41.76	34.40
1990	133.72	123.53	98.66	93.03	123.53	96.79	84.94	64.47	66.06
CEREALS									
1952					25.38	20.68	17.42	16.30	15.40
1955					25.13	20.06	17.62	16.48	15.58
1960					28.37	23.38	21.21	19.43	18.75
1965					32.91	26.62	23.83	22.33	21.41
1970					37.87	32.85	29.44	28.24	27.16
1975	68.88	63.41	61.79	54.66	63.41	58.68	53.09	52.45	50.68
1980	128.60	118.41	108.63	99.57	118.41	115.45	102.76	102.90	101.57
1985	177.30	158.55	147.85	140.30	158.55	146.00	134.67	118.21	113.43
1990	237.61	219.99	211.63	201.98	219.99	206.90	199.70	167.46	165.10
BEVERAGES									
1952					6.10	4.10	3.60	3.04	2.70
1955					11.01	7.60	6.11	5.29	4.48
1960					10.23	7.47	6.02	5.13	4.37
1965					10.19	7.48	5.73	5.07	4.19
1970					12.10	8.47	6.93	5.73	5.52
1975	19.92	15.46	13.69	13.06	15.46	10.64	9.05	7.98	7.63
1980	45.34	37.70	33.31	27.83	37.70	26.43	20.59	18.94	17.06
1985	62.71	55.85	50.17	45.15	55.85	39.29	30.74	26.46	18.83
1990	65.57	57.15	47.64	47.68	57.15	38.05	30.30	30.92	25.37
TOTAL									
1952					142.48	109.56	93.55	82.23	73.73
1955					180.64	136.35	112.60	99.66	84.96
1960					201.19	153.32	129.94	111.84	98.67
1965					230.42	179.19	150.82	133.03	114.24
1970					281	215	182	165	150
1975	468	457	442	388	457	387	329	308	285
1980	862	869	802	742	869	753	626	585	536
1985	1138	1115	1039	931	1115	892	803	695	591
1990	1443	1452	1338	1261	1452	1237	1035	894	870

(a) Until 1970, data shown relate to households containing one adult of each sex and excludes households containing adolescents (aged 15 - 17 years)

(b) Until 1970, includes only households where both adults are aged under 55.

(c) Tomatoes are included with Fruit prior to 1975.

Table 8
Nutritional value of household foods, national averages 1940 to 1990

	Energy (MJ)	Energy (kcal)	Fat (g)	Fatty acids Saturated (g)	Mono unsaturated (g)	Poly unsaturated (g)	P/S Ratio	Protein Total (g)	Animal (g)	Vegetable (g)	Carbo-hydrate (g)	Fibre (g)	% Energy from Fat	Protein	Carbo-hydrate
1940	9.9	2,355						77	35	42				13.1	
1941	9.8	2,339						73	29	44				12.5	
1942	9.5	2,269						74	34	40				13.1	
1943	9.5	2,272	86					73	34	39	301		34.1	12.9	53.0
1944	10.0	2,387	94					73	35	38	311		35.4	12.2	52.1
1945	9.9	2,375	92					76	35	41	309		34.9	12.8	52.0
1946	9.7	2,307	86					78	37	41	305		33.6	13.5	52.9
1947	9.7	2,308	82					77	36	41	315		32.0	13.3	54.6
1948	10.0	2,387	88					77	34	43	322		33.2	12.9	53.9
1949	10.1	2,425	95					76	34	42	316		35.3	12.5	52.2
1950	10.3	2,474	101					78	38	40	314		36.7	12.6	50.7
1951	10.3	2,465	97					77	37	40	321		35.4	12.5	52.2
1952	10.2	2,447	94					77	38	39	324		34.5	12.6	52.9
1953	10.5	2,520	101					78	40	38	325		36.0	12.4	51.6
1954	11.0	2,626	107					77	41	36	340		36.5	11.7	51.8
1955	11.1	2,641	107					77	42	35	342		36.6	11.6	51.7
1956	11.1	2,660	111					75.1	42.7	32.4	364		37.4	11.3	51.2
1957	11.0	2,620	113					74.1	42.7	31.4	351		38.7	11.3	50.1
1958	11.0	2,630	114					74.1	42.7	31.9	351		38.5	11.3	50.0
1959	11.0	2,620	113	53.0	43.0	9.2	0.17	73.2	42.7	30.5	350		38.8	11.2	50.1
1960	11.0	2,630	115					74.7	44.1	30.6	345		39.3	11.4	49.3
1961	11.0	2,630	116					75.1	44.9	30.2	343		39.6	11.4	49.0
1962	11.1	2,640	117					73.3	45.7	29.6	342		40.0	11.4	48.6
1963	11.1	2,650	118					76.5	46.0	30.5	343		39.8	11.5	48.5
1964	10.9	2,600	116					75.1	45.1	30.0	333		40.3	11.6	48.0
1965	10.8	2,590	116					75.2	45.5	29.7	332		40.4	11.6	47.9
1966	10.7	2,560	117					75.6	46.3	29.3	321		41.0	11.8	47.0
1967	10.8	2,590	119					75.8	46.7	29.1	324		41.3	11.7	47.0
1968	10.7	2,560	118					75.4	46.6	28.8	318		41.6	11.8	46.6
1969	10.8	2,570	120	56.7	46.5	11.0	0.19	74.4	46.5	27.9	317		42.0	11.6	46.3
1970	10.7	2,560	119					73.7	45.5	28.2	317		41.8	11.5	46.5
1971	10.4	2,490	117					72.4	45.1	27.3	305		42.3	11.6	46.0
1972	10.2	2,430	112	52.0	42.9	11.5	0.22	72.5	44.7	27.8	301		41.5	11.9	46.4
1973	10.0	2,400	111	51.5	41.9	11.5	0.22	71.4	44.5	26.9	293		42.0	12.0	46.0
1974	9.7	2,320	106	50.7	39.8	10.6	0.20	70.9	44.8	26.1	287		41.3	12.3	46.4
1975	9.6	2,290	107	51.7	39.8	10.1	0.19	72.0	45.8	26.1	275		42.2	12.6	45.2
1976	9.6	2,280	105	50.1	39.7	10.5	0.20	72.3	46.0	26.0	277		41.7	12.7	45.7
1977	9.5	2,260	105	47.5	39.0	10.4	0.21	72.6	46.3	26.0	273		41.9	12.8	45.3
1978	9.5	2,250	106	47.2	39.3	10.6	0.22	73.4	46.3	26.3	272		42.0	12.9	45.1
1979	9.5	2,250	106	47.8	39.7	10.7	0.22	73.4	47.2	25.2	268		42.4	13.0	44.6
1980	9.4	2,230	106	46.8	39.6	11.3	0.24	72.7	46.7	26.0	264		42.6	13.0	44.4
1981	9.3	2,210	104	45.6	38.9	11.4	0.25	71.5	45.6	25.9	264		42.2	12.9	44.9
1982	9.1	2,180	103	44.4	38.7	12.1	0.27	70.0	44.8	25.2	258		42.6	12.9	44.5
1983	9.0	2,140	101	44.5	37.0	12.8	0.29	69.7	44.1	25.6	253		42.6	13.0	44.3
1984	8.7	2,060	97	41.9	35.1	12.7	0.30	67.6	42.4	25.2	246		42.3	13.1	44.6
1985	8.5	2,020	96	40.6	34.7	13.1	0.32	67.4	41.9	25.5	238		42.6	13.3	44.1
1986	8.7	2,070	98	40.6	35.8	14.3	0.35	69.3	42.9	26.4	244	13.0	42.6	13.4	44.0
1987	8.6	2,040	96	39.4	34.8	14.5	0.36	68.7	42.4	26.3	241	12.7	42.2	13.5	44.3
1988	8.4	2,000	93	38.3	33.8	14.2	0.37	67.8	41.9	25.9	237	12.5	42.0	13.6	44.4
1989	8.1	1,940	90	36.9	33.1	13.6	0.37	65.9	40.8	25.0	230	12.4	41.9	13.6	44.5
1990	7.9	1,872	86	34.6	31.8	13.9	0.40	63.1	38.7	24.4	224	12.1	41.6	12.6	44.9

Table 8 *continued*

per person per day

	Calcium (mg)	Iron (mg)	Sodium (g)	Thiamin (mg)	Ribo-flavin (mg)	Nicotinic acid (mg)	Nicotinic acid equiv. (mg)	Vitamin[a] C (mg)	Vitamin[b] A (iu)	Retinol (µg)	β- Carotene (µg)	Vitamin D (µg)
1940	614	12.8		1.18	1.49	12.3		(51)				2.93
1941	605	12.4		1.18	1.40	11.9		(39)				2.40
1942	672	13.5		1.40	1.59	11.9		38	2,982			2.50
1943	855	13.3		1.55	1.64	12.7		40	3,071			2.80
1944	868	13.5		1.62	1.76	13.9		40	3,173			2.65
1945	875	12.7		1.47	1.58	13.2		43	2,908			3.57
1946	912	14.4		1.55	1.65	14.5		44	2,926			3.43
1947	996	14.3		1.52	1.64	12.9		44	2,929			3.13
1948	1,012	14.2		1.57	1.65	12.8		51	3,143			3.50
1949	1,030	13.6		1.53	1.64	12.7		49	3,146			3.25
1950	1,066	13.6		1.51	1.69	13.0		(43)	3,536			4.30
1951	1,076	12.8		1.33	1.59	12.5		(50)	3,432			3.93
1952	1,043	13.0		1.28	1.64	12.9		53	3,551			3.70
1953	1,040	13.3		1.31	1.66	13.3		53	3,836			3.47
1954	1,034	13.4		1.28	1.67	13.3		50	3,911			3.60
1955	1,044	13.5		1.24	1.65	13.1		51	4,199			3.60
1956	1,030	13.3		1.21	1.65	13.0		50	4,310			3.75
1957	1,030	14.1		1.29	1.66	13.8		52	4,290			3.63
1958	1,040	14.2		1.25	1.64	13.6		49	4,350			3.33
1959	1,030	13.9		1.27	1.65	13.8		52	4,280			3.63
1960	1,040	14.1		1.27	1.70	14.0		52	4,360			3.25
1961	1,040	14.2		1.26	1.70	13.9		51	4,320			3.20
1962	1,030	14.2		1.26	1.72	13.8		50	4,310			3.15
1963	1,050	14.4		1.28	1.75	14.0		49	4,420			3.17
1964	1,030	14.1		1.26	1.71	13.7		51	4,420			3.25
1965	1,020	13.9		1.27	1.70	13.9		52	4,370			3.13
1966	1,020	13.6		1.24	1.83	15.8	29.0	53	1,420			3.16
1967	1,040	14.0		1.22	1.81	15.7	29.0	52	1,440			3.24
1968	1,040	13.5		1.21	1.81	15.7	29.0	52	1,440			3.14
1969	1,050	13.3		1.17	1.79	16.2	29.4	52	1,360	910	2,110	2.90
1970	1,030	13.4		1.17	1.77	16.1	29.4	52	1,350	890	2,120	2.82
1971	1,020	13.3		1.18	1.75	16.2	28.9	53	1,340	880	2,140	2.78
1972	1,010	13.2		1.26	1.78	16.6	29.3	52	1,340	890	2,120	2.91
1973	1,020	12.7		1.22	1.79	16.6	29.0	53	1,270	810	2,180	2.89
1974	1,010	11.6		1.15	1.74	15.7	28.5	50	1,230	770	2,150	2.66
1975	1,010	11.6		1.15	1.77	16.0	28.9	51	1,370	930	2,050	2.63
1976	1,010	11.5		1.16	1.77	16.0	28.7	48	1,480	1,020	2,210	2.69
1977	1,000	11.0		1.23	1.81	16.1	29.1	52	1,470	1,030	2,160	2.65
1978	990	11.2		1.19	1.95	16.5	29.5	54	1,490	1,000	2,370	2.65
1979	960	11.0		1.22	1.90	15.9	30.6	54	1,350	970	2,320	2.72
1980	960	11.3		1.16	1.92	14.2	29.6	58	1,350	960	2,360	2.85
1981	950	10.9		1.15	1.87	13.9	29.1	59	1,340	960	2,320	2.99
1982	940	10.9		1.16	1.74	13.6	28.4	57	1,400	1,020	2,280	2.96
1983	880	11.1		1.24	1.76	13.8	28.7	57	1,300	920	2,260	2.96
1984	860	11.1		1.26	1.77	13.7	28.4	55	1,380	1,020	2,140	2.92
1985	850	10.8	2.60	1.33	1.76	12.3	27.0	52	1,370	1,000	2,260	2.96
1986	890	11.3	2.67	1.39	1.82	13.1	28.0	60	1,370	970	2,160	3.24
1987	870	11.1	2.63	1.35	1.78	12.8	27.3	60	1,330	920	2,120	3.18
1988	860	10.9	2.63	1.39	1.68	12.9	27.4	61	1,270	877	2,375	3.09
1989	840	10.6	2.59	1.32	1.64	12.3	26.4	54	1,220	815	2,445	3.04
1990	820	10.4	2.50	1.28	1.61	11.7	25.1	52	1,100	783	1,877	3.02

(a) Values in parentheses are estimates to includes cooking losses.
(b) Values for 1966 onwards are as µg of retinol equivalent.

115

Glossary

Glossary of terms used in the Survey

Adult   A person of 18 years of age or over; however, solely for purposes of classifying households according to their composition, heads of household and diary-keepers under 18 years of age are regarded as adults.

Average consumption   The aggregate amount of food obtained for consumption (q.v.) by the households in the sample divided by the total number of persons in the sample.

Average expenditure   The aggregate amount spent by the households in the sample divided by the total number of persons in the sample.

Average price   Sometimes referred to as 'average unit value'.   The aggregate expenditure by the households in the sample on an item in the Survey Classification of foods, divided by the aggregate quantity of that item purchased by those households.

Child   A person under 18 years of age; however, solely for purposes of classifying households according to their composition, heads of household and diary-keepers under 18 years of age are regarded as adults.

Convenience foods   Those processed foods for which the degree of preparation has been carried to an advanced stage by the manufacturer and which may be used as labour-saving alternatives to less highly processed products. The convenience foods distinguished by the Survey are cooked and canned meats, meat products (other than uncooked sausages), cooked and canned fish, fish products, canned vegetables, vegetable products, canned fruit, fruit juices, cakes and pastries, biscuits, breakfast cereals, puddings (including canned milk puddings), cereal products, instant coffee and coffee essences, baby foods, canned soups, dehydrated soups, icecream, and all frozen foods which fulfil the requirements of the previous sentence.

Food obtained for consumption   Food purchases from all sources (including purchases in bulk) made by households during their week of participation in the Survey and intended for human consumption during that week or later, plus any garden or allotment produce etc (q.v.) which households actually consumed while participating in the Survey, but excluding sweets, alcohol, soft drinks and meals or snacks purchased to eat outside the home. For an individual household, the quantity of food thus obtained for consumption, or estimates of nutrient intake derived from it, may differ from actual consumption because of changes in household stocks during the week and because of wastage. Averaged over a sufficiently large group of households and a sufficiently long period of time household stock increases might reasonably be expected to differ but little from household stock depletions provided other things remain equal.

Garden and allotment produce, etc   Food which enters the household without payment, for consumption during the week of participation in the Survey; it includes supplies obtained from a garden, allotment or farm, or from an employer, but not gifts of food from one household in Great Britain to another if such food has been purchased by the donating household. (See also 'Value of garden and allotment produced, etc').

Household   For the Survey purposes, this is defined as a group of persons living in the same dwelling and sharing common catering arrangements.

Income group   Households are grouped into eight income groups (A1, A2, B, C, D, E1, E2 and OAP) according to the ascertained or estimated gross income of the head of the household, or of the principal earner in the household if the weekly income of the head is less than the amount defining the upper limit to income group D.

Intake   *See* 'Food obtained for consumption.'

Net balance   The net balance of an individual (a member of the household or a visitor) is a measure of the number of meals eaten in the home by that individual during the Survey week, each meal being given a weight in proportion to its importance. The relative weights are breakfast 3, dinner (mid-day) 4, tea 2 and supper 5. The weights for tea and supper are interchanged according to whichever of the two meals is the larger; if only one evening meal is taken it is given a relative weight of 7. The net balance is used when relating nutrient intake to need.

Nutrients   In addition to the energy value of food expressed in terms of kilocalories and megajoules (4,184 megajoules = 1,000 kilocalories), the food is evaluated in terms of the following nutrients:

> Protein (animal and total), fat (including the component saturated, mono-unsaturated and polyunsaturated fatty acids), carbohydrate, calcium, iron, sodium, vitamin A (retinol, β-carotene, retinol equivalent), thiamin, riboflavin, niacin (total, tryptophan, niacin equivalent), vitamins C and D, dietary fibre and sugars.

Separate figures for animal and total protein are included; as a generalisation, foods of animal origin are of greater nutritional value than those of vegetable origin because of a greater content of some B vitamins and trace elements, so that the proportion of animal protein is to some extent an indication of the nutritive value of the diet.

Pensioner households (OAP)   Households in which at least three-quarters of total income is derived from national insurance retirement of similar pensions and/or supplementary pensions or allowances paid in supplementation or instead of such pensions. Such households will include at least one person over the national insurance retirement age.

117

Person An individual of any age who during the week of the Survey spends at least four nights in the household ('at home') and has at least one meal a day from the household food supply on at least four days, except that if he/she is the head of the household, or the diary-keeper, he or she is regarded as a person in all cases.

Price index A price index of Fisher 'Ideal' type is used; this index is the geometric mean of two indices with weights appropriate to the earlier and later periods respectively, or in the case of non-temporal comparisons (eg regional, type of area, income group and household composition), with weights appropriate to the group under consideration and the national average respectively.

Real price The price of an item of food in relation to the price of all goods and services. The term is used when referring to changes in the price of an item over a period of time. It is measured by dividing the average price (q.v.) paid at a point in time by the General Index of Retail Prices (all items) at that time.

Regions The standard regions for statistical purposes, except that East Anglia is combined with the South East region; *see* Table 1 of Appendix A.

Seasonal foods Those foods which regularly exhibit a marked seasonal variation in price or in consumption; these are (for the purposes of the Survey) eggs, fresh and processed fish, shellfish, potatoes, fresh vegetables and fresh fruit.

Value of consumption Expenditure plus value of garden and allotment produce, etc (q.v.)

Value of garden and allotment produce, etc The value imputed to such supplies received by a group of households is derived from the average prices currently paid by the group for corresponding purchases. This appears to be the only practicable method of valuing these supplies, though if the households concerned had not had access to them, they would probably not have replaced them fully by purchases at retail prices, and would therefore have spent less than estimated value of their consumption. Free school milk and free welfare milk are valued at the average price paid by the group for full price milk. (*See also* 'Garden and allotment produce, etc').

Symbols and conventions used

Symbols   The following are used throughout -

    – = nil

    ... = less than half the final digit shown

na or blank = not available or not applicable

Rounding of figures   In tables where figures have been rounded to the nearest final digit, there may therefore be an apparent slight discrepancy between the sum of the constituent items and the total shown.

Additional Information

Analyses of Survey data providing more detail and, in some cases, more-up-to-date information than published in this report are available directly from the Ministry of Agriculture, Fisheries and Food.

Standard analyses
    quarterly national averages - available approximately 10 weeks after the
    end of each survey period
    analyses of components of selected food codes

Ad hoc Analyses
    Ad hoc analyses can be undertaken to meet the special requirements of
    organisations subject to resources being available

Further details regarding additional Survey information are available from:

National Food Survey Branch
Ministry of Agriculture, Fisheries and Food
Room 513, West Block
Whitehall Place
London SW1A 2HH

Telephone: 071-270-8562/3